THE EVERYDAY AIR FRYER COOKBOOK

Fast, Nutritious Recipes Perfect for Busy British Kitchens with the Metric Measurements | Full Colour Edition

Cristi G. Piedra

Copyright© 2024 By Cristi G. Piedra Rights Reserved

This book is copyright protected. It is only for personal use. You cannot amend, distribute, sell, use, quote or paraphrase any part of the content within this book, without the consent of the author or publisher.

Under no circumstances will any blame or legal responsibility be held against the publisher, or author, for any damages, reparation, or monetary loss due to the information contained within this book, either directly or indirectly.

Limit of Liability/Disclaimer of Warranty:

No book, including this one, can ever replace the diagnostic expertise and medical advice of a physician in providing information about your health. The information contained herein is not intended to replace medical advice. You should consult with your doctor before using the information in this or any health-related book.

The Publisher and the author make no representations or warranties with respect to the accuracy or completeness of the contents of this work and specifically disclaim all warranties, including without limitation warranties of fitness for a particular purpose. No warranty may be created or extended by sales or promotional materials. The advice and strategies contained herein may not be suitable for every situation. This work is sold with the understanding that the Publisher is not engaged in rendering medical, legal, or other professional advice or services. If professional assistance is required, the services of a competent professional person should be sought. Neither the Publisher nor the author shall be liable for damages arising here from. The fact that an individual, organization, or website is referred to in this work as a citation and/or potential source of further information does not mean that the author or the Publisher endorses the information the individual, organization, or website may provide or recommendations they/it may make. Further, readers should be aware that websites listed in this work may have changed or disappeared between when this work was written and when it is read.

Manufactured in the United Kingdom
Interior and Cover Designer: Danielle Rees
Art Producer: Brooke White
Editor: Aaliyah Lyons
Production Editor: Sienna Adams
Production Manager: Sarah Johnson
Photography: Michael Smith

TABLE OF CONTENTS

Introduction — 1

Chapter 1: The Air Fryer Adventure — 2

    The Air Fryer Revolution — 2
    Why We Love It — 3
    Tips for Success — 4
    Air Fryer Cooking Chart — 6

Chapter 2: Appetizers & Small Bites — 8

    Spinach-Feta Arancini — 9
    Mozzarella Sticks — 9
    Fried Buffalo Wings — 10
    Butternut Bites — 10
    Jalapeño Poppers — 11
    Chicken Wings & Blue Cheese Dip — 11
    Goats' Cheese Toasts with Walnuts — 12
    Sage and Onion Stuffing Balls — 12
    Cheesy Potato Skins — 13
    Cheesy Dipping Sticks — 13

Chapter 3: Morning Delights — 14

    Full English Breakfast — 15
    Courgette & Sweetcorn Fritters — 15
    Parma Ham Turnovers — 16
    Fruity Granola — 16
    Soft-Boiled Eggs & Soldiers — 17
    Sweet Potato Hash — 17
    Sausage & Egg Breakfast Muffin — 18
    Apricot & Almond Pastries — 18
    Stuffed Pepper Breakfast Omelette — 19

TABLE OF CONTENTS

    Marmalade & Seed Muffins — 19

Chapter 4: Meat Lover's Paradise — 20

    Stir Fried Pork and Leek — 21
    Lamb Kofta Wraps — 21
    Bacon and Broccoli Quiche Cups — 22
    Pork & Apple Burgers — 22
    Tonnato Steak — 23
    Fruity Pork Steaks — 24
    Spiced Pork Fillets — 24
    Shepherd's Pie — 25
    Bacon and Turkey Burger Bites — 26
    Country Fried Pork Chops — 26

Chapter 5: Chicken and Fish Dishes — 27

    Beetroot Side of Salmon — 28
    London Fried Fish — 28
    Super-Crispy Chicken Schnitzel — 29
    Tuna Pasta Bake — 30
    Fish Pie — 30
    Chicken Massaman Curry — 31
    A Whole Chicken — 31
    Pineapple & Piri Piri Turkey Burgers — 32
    Turkey Satay — 33
    Beer-Battered Fish and Chips — 33

Chapter 6: Vegetable-Based Creations — 34

    Crispy Butternut Squash Gnocchi — 35
    Potato Cakes — 35
    Mushroom Burgers & Traditional Coleslaw — 36
    Mediterranean-Style Air-Fried Vegetables — 36

TABLE OF CONTENTS

Spiced Cauliflower Steaks	37
Creamy Mushroom Stroganoff	37
Rainbow Brunch Bowl	38
Courgette and Feta Balls	38
Teriyaki Vegetables	39
Summer Vegetable Gratin	39

Chapter 7: Tasty Sides and Snacks — 40

Cheese-Stuffed Portobello Mushrooms	41
Parmesan Chicken Wings	41
Crispy Potato Wedges	42
Chocolate Velvet Cake	42
Perfect Potato Pancakes	43
Sweet, Salt, Or Butter Popcorn	43
Pecan Pie Baked Oats	44
Sweet 'N' Spicy Sweet-Potato Chips	44
Baked Goat's Cheese Pots	45
Chilli and Paprika Root Vegetable Crisps	45

Chapter 8: Classical & Simple — 46

Garlic Prawn Starter	47
Squash with Blue Cheese Dressing	47
Garlic Butter Salmon with Green Beans	48
Garlic Bread	48
Roasted Beets and Parsnips with Tahini Dressing	49
Fried Olives	49
Veggie Burgers	50
Caribbean Bone-Free Jackfruit "Pork" Chops	50
Courgette Pizza Slices	51
Charred Corn Salsa Salad	51

TABLE OF CONTENTS

Chapter 9: Weekend Feasts — 52

- Orzo with Prawns & Salsa Verde — 53
- Tandoori Chicken breast fillet — 53
- The Complete Air Fried Barbecue — 54
- Buttermilk-Marinated Roast Chicken — 55
- Dom's Weeknight Meat Pizza — 55
- Family Favourites Roast Lamb — 56
- Marinaded Filipino-Style Barbecue Chicken — 56
- Chilli Con Carne — 57
- Sticky Pork Ribs with Honey and Garlic — 57
- Classic Bangers and Mash with Onion Gravy — 58

Chapter 10: Sauces & Homemade Essentials — 59

- Roasted Aubergine Mediterraneo — 60
- Spicy Ketchup — 60
- Honey Mustard Sauce — 61
- Sweet and Sour Sauce — 61
- Spicy Garlic Parmesan Sauce — 61
- BBQ Sauce — 61
- Basic Homemade Breadcrumbs — 62
- Sour Cream & Bacon Dip — 62
- Homemade Garlic Butter — 62
- Creamy Ranch Sauce — 62

Appendix 1: Measurement Conversion Chart — 63

Appendix 2: The Dirty Dozen and Clean Fifteen — 64

Appendix 3: Index — 65

INTRODUCTION

I'll be honest; I never thought I'd become the proud owner of an air fryer, but here we are! It's turned into our secret weapon in the kitchen, especially with a busy family like ours. Between work, school, and everything else, finding time to whip up healthy meals can be a challenge, but the air fryer has made it so much easier.

On busy mornings, it's become our go-to gadget. Just the other day, I was up at the crack of dawn, trying to prepare breakfast for my family. While the coffee brewed, I tossed some diced sweet potatoes into the air fryer with a sprinkle of olive oil and paprika. In less than 20 minutes, we had crispy sweet potato cubes ready to go. My husband and I enjoyed them in wraps, while my teenage daughter, ever the independent spirit, had her heart set on making fries for herself. With a quick tutorial from me, she took over, tossing the frozen fries into the fryer. I was amazed to see her working the machine like a pro!

Family gatherings are another highlight. We often gather on weekends, and the air fryer is the star of the show. From crispy chicken wings to roasted veggies, we've made so many delicious meals. Everyone loves the crunchiness, and best of all, I feel good knowing we're keeping things healthier.

I never imagined something so simple could make cooking so enjoyable for my family. The air fryer has not only saved us time but also brought us together in the kitchen. Who knew I'd find joy in cooking again?

DEDICATION

I want to take a moment to express my heartfelt gratitude to my daughter Ava. Her skill with the air fryer has truly been a game changer for our family. Not only has she made cooking easier for me, but her enthusiasm has also sparked my creativity in the kitchen. When she suggested that I share the new recipes we've successfully developed, it inspired me to create this book. Ava's angelic presence brings so much joy and innovation to our home, and I'm thankful every day for her support and inspiration. I hope these recipes bring happiness to your kitchen, too!

CHAPTER 1: THE AIR FRYER ADVENTURE

THE AIR FRYER REVOLUTION

WHAT IS AN AIR FRYER?

An air fryer is a compact kitchen appliance that uses hot air circulation to cook food, simulating the results of deep frying without the excess oil. Imagine a mini convection oven that can quickly crisping up your meals! The technology behind it involves a powerful fan that circulates hot air around the food, allowing it to cook evenly and develop a delightful crunch. It's a game-changer for anyone looking to enjoy fried foods without the guilt. Plus, most air fryers are user-friendly, featuring preset functions that make cooking a breeze, even for beginners.

HEALTHIER COOKING OPTIONS

One of the standout benefits of the air fryer is its ability to create healthier meals. Traditional frying methods require a significant amount of oil, which adds extra calories and unhealthy fats. In contrast, air frying typically requires little to no oil, helping you cut down on those unwanted calories. For instance, you can achieve perfectly crispy Chips with just a tablespoon of oil—or none at all! The reduced oil not only makes meals lighter but also helps retain the nutrients in your ingredients. This means you can enjoy your favourite comfort foods while staying on track with your health goals.

Additionally, the air fryer can cook a variety of foods that may not usually be fried, like vegetables and fish, giving you the freedom to explore new healthy recipes. Roasting a batch of Brussels sprouts or air-frying salmon can result in delicious, nutrient-rich meals that taste fantastic without compromising on health.

VERSATILITY BEYOND FRYING

One of the most appealing aspects of the air fryer is its versatility. While it's often celebrated for its frying capabilities, it can do much more than that. The air fryer can bake, roast, and grill, making it an all-in-one cooking solution for your kitchen.

Want to whip up a batch of muffins for breakfast? No problem! The air fryer can bake them to perfection in a fraction of the time it would take in a conventional oven. Craving roasted veggies? Toss them in the air fryer for perfectly caramelized bites that are crispy on the outside and tender on the inside. Even pizza can be made in the air fryer, giving you a crispy crust in just minutes.

Grilling is another fantastic feature; you can achieve those lovely grill marks on meats and vegetables without firing up the barbecue. This is especially convenient during colder months when outdoor grilling isn't feasible.

Plus, the air fryer is great for reheating leftovers, bringing them back to life with that fresh-out-of-the-oven taste. No more soggy microwaved meals; the air fryer will crisp them up, making them just as enjoyable the second time around.

WHY WE LOVE IT

QUICK MEAL PREP

In today's fast-paced world, time is a luxury many of us can't afford, especially when it comes to meal prep. This is where the air fryer shines. With its rapid cooking capabilities, it transforms how we approach weeknight dinners. Gone are the days of waiting for the oven to preheat or dealing with multiple pans on the hob.

Air fryers heat up in minutes, meaning you can toss in your ingredients and have a meal ready in a fraction of the time. For example, frozen chicken tenders that would take ages to bake can be done in about 15 minutes in the air fryer. It's perfect for those hectic evenings when you're juggling work, kids, and everything else life throws at you. And because air fryers cook food quickly, you can experiment with different ingredients and recipes without worrying about spending hours in the kitchen.

The convenience extends beyond dinner, too. If you're someone who loves meal prepping for the week, the air fryer can help you whip up big batches of roasted vegetables or proteins in no time, making healthy eating that much easier.

EASY CLEAN-UP

Let's be real—clean-up is often the worst part of cooking. But with an air fryer, that's a problem of the past. Most models feature non-stick surfaces that prevent food from sticking, making it super easy to wipe down after use. Plus, many air fryer baskets and trays are dishwasher-safe, meaning you can pop them in the dishwasher without a second thought.

This ease of clean-up encourages you to use your air fryer more often. You won't hesitate to make a quick snack or side dish when you know the mess won't take forever to tackle afterward. Whether it's fries, veggies, or even a whole chicken, the air fryer simplifies the cooking process and the subsequent clean-up, leaving you with more time to relax.

CHAPTER 1

CONSISTENT RESULTS

Another reason we love the air fryer is its ability to deliver consistently great results. Unlike traditional frying, where the heat can vary, the air fryer uses convection technology to circulate hot air evenly around your food. This ensures that everything cooks uniformly, resulting in that perfect golden-brown finish we all crave.

Imagine making a batch of crispy potato wedges; with an air fryer, you can expect them to be evenly cooked and crunchy every time. No more burnt edges or undercooked centres! This consistency is especially beneficial for beginner cooks who may be unsure about cooking times and temperatures. The air fryer takes the guesswork out of cooking, making it easier to achieve professional-level results at home.

Additionally, many air fryers come with preset cooking modes for popular dishes, making it even simpler to get things right. Just select the type of food you're cooking, and the air fryer will automatically adjust the time and temperature for you. This feature is a huge confidence booster for anyone looking to expand their cooking repertoire.

TIPS FOR SUCCESS

PREHEATING FOR PERFECTION

When it comes to using an air fryer, one simple step can make all the difference: preheating. Just like with a traditional oven, preheating your air fryer is essential for achieving optimal results. It ensures that your food starts cooking immediately at the right temperature, leading to that desired crispiness and golden-brown finish.

Most air fryers heat up quickly, usually within 3-5 minutes. Simply set your temperature and allow it to warm up before adding your food. This step is particularly crucial for items like frozen foods, which benefit from that initial blast of heat. For example, when you preheat before tossing in those frozen chips, they'll cook evenly, giving you that perfect crunch instead of a soggy texture.

Skipping this step can lead to uneven cooking, with some parts of your food being overcooked while others remain underdone. So, take the extra few minutes to preheat, and you'll be rewarded with consistently delicious results.

BATCH COOKING MADE EASY

If you're feeding a crowd or just want to meal prep for the week, batch cooking in the air fryer can be a game changer. With its generous capacity, you can easily prepare multiple portions at once, saving you time and effort.

Start by grouping similar foods together for efficient cooking. For instance, if you're making roasted veggies, try combining peppers, courgette, and carrots in one batch. The key is to cut them into similar sizes to ensure they cook evenly. A little bit of oil and your favourite seasonings will enhance the flavours without requiring much extra work.

THE AIR FRYER ADVENTURE

If you have a larger air fryer, consider cooking proteins and sides simultaneously. You could air-fry chicken breast fillets on one side while roasting broccoli on the other. Just be mindful of cooking times; some items may need to be removed earlier than others.

And don't forget about leftovers! Batch cooking means you can easily make extra portions of your meals, ensuring you have healthy options ready to go for those busy days. Just store them in the fridge or freezer, and reheat them in the air fryer for a quick and satisfying meal.

EXPERIMENTING WITH FLAVOURS

One of the best parts about cooking with an air fryer is the opportunity to experiment with flavours. Don't be afraid to get creative with seasonings, marinades, and sauces. Air frying is an excellent way to enhance the natural taste of your ingredients while adding a kick of flavour.

Start with the basics: olive oil, salt, and pepper. From there, you can explore various herbs and spices. Think garlic powder, paprika, or Italian seasoning for a deliciously aromatic twist. For meats, marinades can take your dishes to the next level. A quick soak in a marinade of soy sauce, ginger, and honey can turn a simple chicken breast fillet into a flavourful delight.

For a fun challenge, try creating your own spice blends. Mixing cumin, coriander leaf, and cayenne can give your roasted veggies a lovely warmth. Or, for a sweet treat, toss some apple slices with cinnamon and a touch of brown sugar before air frying for a tasty pudding.

Also, consider trying out international flavours! Asian, Mediterranean, or Mexican spices can completely transform your meals and keep things interesting. The air fryer allows the spices to adhere beautifully to your food, creating a delightful crust that makes every bite a burst of flavour.

CHAPTER 1

AIR FRYER COOKING CHART

Food	Temperature (°C)	Cooking Time (minutes)
Chips (thin)	200	10-15
Chips (thick)	200	15-20
Chicken wings	180	20-25
Chicken breast fillet	180	15-20
Salmon fillet	200	8-10
Shrimp	200	8-10
Onion rings	200	8-10
Vegetables (broccoli, etc.)	180	10-15
Frozen vegetables (mix)	180	10-15
Breaded fish fillets	200	10-12
Hamburgers	200	8-10
Bacon	180	6-8
Sausages	180	12-15
Meatballs	180	12-15
Baked potatoes	200	45-50
Sweet potatoes	200	20-25
Chicken breast fillets	200	15-20 min
Chicken thighs	200	20-25 min
Chicken wings	200	18-20 min
Fish fillets	200	8-12 min
Shrimp	200	6-8 min
Scallops	200	6-8 min
Salmon	200	10-12 min
Pork chops	200	12-15 min
Pork tenderloin	200	20-25 min
Steak (1 inch thick)	200	8-10 min
Hamburger patties	200	8-10 min
Hot dogs/sausages	200	6-8 min

Food	Temperature (°C)	Cooking Time (minutes)
Chips	200	15-20 min
Sweet potato fries	200	15-20 min
Potato wedges	200	15-20 min
Onion rings	200	12-15 min
Courgette/squash fries	200	10-12 min
Broccoli/cauliflower	200	8-10 min
Brussel sprouts	200	12-15 min
Carrots	200	12-15 min
Asparagus	200	6-8 min
Corn on the cob	200	12-15 min
Baked potatoes	200	40-45 min
Stuffed mushrooms	200	8-10 min
Roasted peppers	200	8-10 min
Chicken nuggets	200	10-12 min
Meatballs	200	10-12 min
Spring rolls	200	10-12 min
Mozzarella sticks	200	6-8 min
Jalapeno poppers	200	8-10 min
Quiche	180	25-30 min
Puff pastry	200	10-12 min
Apple turnovers	200	12-15 min
Chocolate chip cookies	180	6-8 min

Note: Cooking times may vary depending on the type and brand of air fryer, as well as the size and thickness of the food being cooked. Always refer to the manufacturer's instructions and use a food thermometer to ensure that food is cooked to a safe temperature.

CHAPTER 2: APPETIZERS & SMALL BITES

APPETIZERS & SMALL BITES

SPINACH-FETA ARANCINI

Prep time: 10 minutes | **Cook time:** 20 minutes | **Serves** 6

- 1 tbsp olive oil
- 1 large shallot, chopped
- 1 package frozen chopped spinach, thawed and drained
- 50g crumbled feta cheese
- 400g cooked and cooled risotto or short-grain white rice
- 100g plain flour
- 2 large eggs, beaten
- 100g panko breadcrumbs
- Olive oil cooking spray

1. Heat the olive oil in a medium saucepan. Add the shallots and sauté until golden.
2. Add the spinach and sauté with the shallots until the flavors mix, about 2–3 minutes. Drain excess liquid. Stir in the feta and set the mixture aside to cool.
3. Scoop approximately 2 tablespoons of the risotto onto the palm of your hand and flatten.
4. Add about a teaspoon of the spinach-feta filling, then carefully pack into a ball shape. Repeat with the remaining risotto and filling.
5. Roll each of the balls in the flour, then dip into the beaten egg, then roll into the breadcrumbs, coating evenly.
6. Spray each ball with cooking spray before adding to the basket. Air fry at 210°C for 10 minutes per batch, or until golden.

MOZZARELLA STICKS

Prep time: 5 minutes | **Cook time:** 5 minutes | **Serves** 2

- 200g hard mozzarella
- 3 tbsp plain flour
- ¼ tsp salt
- ⅛ tsp black pepper
- 1 large UK egg, beaten
- 25g dried breadcrumbs
- Olive oil spray or 1 tsp olive oil

1. Slice the mozzarella into sticks measuring roughly 1.5 x 1.5 x 5 cm.
2. Place the flour in a bowl with the salt and pepper and stir well. Place the beaten egg in a second bowl and the breadcrumbs in a third. Dip the sticks of cheese first into the flour, then into the beaten egg and then the breadcrumbs. Use a different hand for the egg and breadcrumb procedures. Place these prepared mozzarella sticks on a plate and chill in the freezer for 30 minutes.
3. Preheat the air fryer to 180°C. Add the chilled sticks to the preheated air fryer and spray or drizzle with olive oil. Cook for 4–5 minutes. As soon as you see some of the cheese bubbling out of the breaded coating, they're ready to serve.

CHAPTER 2

FRIED BUFFALO WINGS

Prep time: 10 minutes | Cook time: 30 minutes | Serves 2

- 6 bone-in chicken wings
- 4 tablespoons unsalted butter, melted
- 4 tablespoons hot sauce
- 1 teaspoon apple cider vinegar
- 1 teaspoon soy sauce
- 1 teaspoon ketchup

1. Rinse the wings and pat dry. Section the wings in three parts, discarding the tips. Place the midsections and drumettes in the basket and air fry at 210°C until cooked through, about 25 minutes. Shake the basket 2-3 times during cooking to flip the wings.
2. While the chicken is cooking, prepare the sauce: In a large bowl, whisk together the melted butter, hot sauce, apple cider vinegar, soy sauce, and ketchup.
3. When wings finish cooking, add them to bowl and toss with sauce to coat.

BUTTERNUT BITES

Prep time: 10 minutes | Cook time: 25 minutes | Serves 4

- 1 small butternut squash, peeled and cubed into ½ cm pieces
- 30ml olive oil
- ½ tsp paprika
- ½ tsp garlic powder
- Salt and pepper, to taste

1. In a large bowl, mix olive oil, paprika, garlic powder, salt, and pepper. Add squash cubes and coat evenly.
2. Preheat air fryer to 190°C. Transfer squash and cook for 10 mins.
3. Shake basket, cook for an additional 10-15 mins until tender. Serve warm.

APPETIZERS & SMALL BITES

JALAPEÑO POPPERS

Prep time: 10 minutes | **Cook time:** 10 minutes | **Makes** 14

- 7 jalapeño chillies, halved and deseeded
- 125g cream cheese
- 50g grated mozzarella
- 4 crispy cooked streaky bacon rashers, finely chopped
- 2 spring onions, finely chopped
- 2 tbsp panko breadcrumbs
- ½ tsp smoked paprika
- Olive oil, for spritzing
- Salt and pepper
- Sour cream and chive dip, to serve

1. Cut each jalapeño in half lengthways and use a small spoon to remove the membrane and seeds and discard them. In a bowl, mix together the cream cheese, mozzarella, bacon pieces and spring onions and season to taste. Spoon the cream cheese mixture into the jalapeño halves.
2. Mix the breadcrumbs with the paprika, then dip the cream cheese side of each jalapeño in the breadcrumb mixture.
3. Place the stuffed jalapeños, breadcrumb sides up, in a preheated air fryer, spritz with a little oil and cook at 190°C for 7–8 minutes, until the cheese has melted, the chilli has softened and the topping is crispy. Serve immediately with a ready-made soured cream and chive dip.

CHICKEN WINGS & BLUE CHEESE DIP

Prep time: 10 minutes | **Cook time:** 15 minutes | **Serves** 4

- 500 g chicken wings
- 2 teaspoons olive oil
- 2 teaspoons smoked paprika
- 1 teaspoon garlic powder
- 1 teaspoon onion powder
- salt and pepper

Blue cheese dip

- 50 g soft blue cheese, such as Gorgonzola or dolcelatte
- 75 ml soured cream
- 1 teaspoon lemon juice
- 1 tablespoon chopped chives

1. Place the chicken wings in a bowl, add the olive oil, smoked paprika, garlic powder and onion powder and toss well, so the chicken wings are evenly coated.
2. Cook in a single layer in a preheated air fryer at 200°C for 10 minutes, then turn over and cook for a further 5 minutes, until the skin is crispy and the chicken is cooked through.
3. Meanwhile, mash together all the ingredients for the dip until well combined. Serve the wings with the dip.

CHAPTER 2

GOATS' CHEESE TOASTS WITH WALNUTS

Prep time: 5 minutes | Cook time: 5 minutes | Serves 4

- 4 slices walnut bread
- 1 garlic clove
- 200g soft goats' cheese with rind, cut into 4 slices
- 2 tsp chopped thyme leaves
- 4 walnut halves, chopped
- 4 tsp honey
- Black pepper

To Serve:

- Watercress and halved cherry tomatoes

1. Cook the walnut bread in a preheated air fryer at 180°C for 2 minutes, turning halfway through, until lightly toasted. You may need to do this in 2 batches. Rub the toast all over with the garlic clove.
2. Cut the round of goats' cheese into 4 slices, each about 1.5 cm (¾ inch) thick. Place each slice in the centre of a piece of toast and sprinkle with the thyme leaves, walnuts and pepper. Return to the air fryer and cook for 2–3 minutes, until the cheese starts to melt.
3. Drizzle with the honey and serve immediately with watercress and halved cherry tomatoes.

SAGE AND ONION STUFFING BALLS

Prep time: 10 minutes | Cook time: 15 minutes | Makes 12 medium stuffing balls

- 450g sausage meat
- 20g cold butter, diced
- ½ white onion, diced
- ½ bread roll, chopped
- 2 tbsp dried sage
- Salt and pepper, to taste
- Optional: additional breadcrumbs for binding

1. Chop the bread roll into small chunks.
2. Peel and dice your onion into small pieces.
3. Chop the butter into small chunks.
4. Put all the ingredients with the seasoning in a bowl and mix to combine.
5. Take a tablespoon of mixture and make a medium sized ball, about golf ball sized. Place on a tray and repeat until all the mixture is gone.
6. Place the tray of stuffing balls in the fridge for an hour.
7. A few minutes before you begin cooking, preheat the air fryer to 180°C.
8. Remove the stuffing balls from the fridge, place in the air fryer, and cook for 10 minutes at 180°C.

APPETIZERS & SMALL BITES

CHEESY POTATO SKINS

Prep time: 10 minutes | **Cook time: 50 minutes** | **Serves 4**

- 4 medium red potatoes
- Cooking oil spray
- Salt and pepper, to taste
- 115g Cheddar cheese
- 115g sour cream
- 2 spring onions, sliced thinly

1. Wash/scrub the potatoes thoroughly and pat dry.
2. Preheat air fryer to 200°C.
3. Spray potatoes with cooking oil spray and add salt and pepper to taste.
4. Cook the potatoes in the air fryer at 200°C for about 30–40 minutes. Test the potatoes for readiness with a fork. You should be able to push the fork easily into the potato.
5. One cooked, allow the potatoes to cool enough to handle, then cut them in half and scoop out the inside. Leave a thin layer of potato covering the inside skin.
6. Spray the potatoes again with cooking oil and lay them flat side down in the air fryer.
7. Cook at 200°C for an extra 5 minutes.
8. Open the air fryer enough to sprinkle the Cheddar over the top of the potato skins. Cook for a further 3 minutes until the cheese has melted.
9. Remove the potatoes from the air fryer and serve with sour cream, spring onions and black pepper.

CHEESY DIPPING STICKS

Prep time: 10 minutes | **Cook time: 15 minutes** | **Serves 8**

- 8 cheese sticks
- ½ tsp garlic powder
- ½ tsp smoked paprika
- 1 large egg
- 30g plain flour
- 60g breadcrumbs

1. Place the cheese sticks on a tray in the freezer for 30 minutes.
2. In a bowl, whisk up the egg. In a separate bowl, combine the spices and breadcrumbs. Set the bowls to one side.
3. Put the flour in a resealable plastic food bag.
4. Take the cheese sticks from freezer and cut in half. Place the halves into the bag with the flour. Shake gently to thoroughly cover the cheese sticks with the flour.
5. Dip each cheese stick in egg wash then in the breadcrumbs so that they are thoroughly coated.
6. Return the coated cheese sticks to the freezer for a further 30 minutes.
7. Preheat the air fryer to 190°C.
8. Remove the cheese sticks from the freezer and cook for about 4–5 minutes at 190°C.
9. Once cooked, turn off the heat and allow to rest in the air fryer for a few minutes. Gently reshape with a silicone kitchen utensil.
10. Remove from the air fryer and serve warm with a favourite dipping sauce.

CHAPTER 3: MORNING DELIGHTS

MORNING DELIGHTS

FULL ENGLISH BREAKFAST

Prep time: 10 minutes | **Cook time:** 20 minutes | **Makes** 2

- 4 rashers of back bacon
- 4 pork sausages (e.g., "Cumberland sausages")
- 2 large eggs
- 1 tin (400g) baked beans
- 4 slices of black pudding
- 200g button mushrooms, halved
- 2 tomatoes, halved
- 4 slices of bread (for toast)
- 2 tablespoons butter
- Salt and pepper, to taste
- HP Sauce, to serve (optional)

1. Preheat your air fryer to 200°C.
2. Place the sausages and bacon in the air fryer basket and cook for 10-12 minutes, or until cooked through and crispy. Flip halfway through cooking.
3. Place the black pudding in the air fryer basket and cook for 2-3 minutes per side, or until crisp.
4. Toss the mushrooms and tomatoes with a little olive oil and season with salt and pepper. Place them in the air fryer basket and cook for 5-7 minutes, or until softened.
5. While other ingredients are cooking, heat the beans in a small saucepan over medium heat.
6. While the other ingredients are cooking, fry the eggs in a separate pan to your liking.
7. Toast the bread in a toaster.
8. Arrange the sausages, bacon, black pudding, mushrooms, tomatoes, baked beans, and eggs on a plate. Serve with buttered toast and HP Sauce on the side.

COURGETTE & SWEETCORN FRITTERS

Prep time: 10 minutes | **Cook time:** 10 minutes | **Makes** 8

- 1 large courgette, coarsely grated
- 75 g drained canned sweetcorn
- 1 red chilli, deseeded and finely chopped
- 2 tablespoons chopped mint
- 50 g (2 oz) self-raising flour
- 1 egg, lightly beaten
- 50 g ricotta cheese
- Olive oil, for spritzing
- salt and pepper

To serve

- sweet chilli sauce
- crisp green salad

1. Squeeze the grated courgette in a clean tea towel to remove excess water, then place in a large bowl. Add the sweetcorn, chilli, mint and flour, then stir in the egg. Mix well and season with salt and pepper. Gently fold in the ricotta.
2. Place heaped tablespoons of the batter on a piece of pierced nonstick baking paper in a preheated air fryer, flatten slightly with the back of a spoon and spritz with oil. Cook at 190°C for 6 minutes. Flip over and cook for a further 3–4 minutes, until golden. You may need to do this in 2 batches to make 8 in total.
3. Serve 2 fritters per person, drizzled with a little sweet chilli sauce, with a crisp green salad on the side.

CHAPTER 3

PARMA HAM TURNOVERS

Prep time: 5 minutes | **Cook time:** 30 minutes | **Makes** 6

- 1 × 320g sheet ready-rolled puff pastry
- 3 tablespoons crème fraîche
- 1 tablespoon Dijon mustard
- 6 Parma ham slices
- 100g Cheddar cheese, grated
- 1 egg, lightly beaten

1. Preheat the air fryer to 180°C for 4 minutes.
2. Unroll the pastry sheet and cut it into 6 equal squares. In a small bowl, mix together the crème fraîche and mustard.
3. with a spoon, spread the mustard mix on to each pastry square, spreading it in a line starting from one corner and running diagonally to the opposite corner. Lay a piece of Parma ham over this, then sprinkle over the cheese.
4. Pick up a corner that has no mixture on it and fold into the middle, then repeat with the opposite corner. Repeat to fill and form 6 turnovers.
5. Brush the pastry with some beaten egg and place into the air fryer basket. You may have to do this in batches.
6. Cook for 12 minutes, until risen and golden.

FRUITY GRANOLA

Prep time: 5 minutes | **Cook time:** 25 minutes | **Serves** 4

- 3 tbsp maple syrup or honey
- 1 tbsp sunflower oil
- 200g porridge oats
- 50g pecans, roughly chopped
- 50g almonds, roughly chopped
- 100g mixed seeds (e.g., sunflower, pumpkin, and linseed)
- 1 tsp ground cinnamon
- 100g dried mixed berries (e.g., blueberries, cranberries, strawberries, and cherries)
- To serve: milk or yoghurt, fresh blueberries

1. Heat the maple syrup and oil in a small saucepan over a gentle heat. Place the oats, nuts, seeds and cinnamon in a large bowl and mix well. Pour over the warm maple syrup mixture and stir well to combine.
2. Spread the granola over a piece of pierced nonstick baking paper in a preheated air fryer and cook at 150°C for 20–25 minutes, stirring once, until golden.
3. Remove the granola from the air fryer and allow to cool. Stir in the dried berries and store in an airtight container for up to 4 weeks. Serve with milk or yogurt and fresh blueberries.

MORNING DELIGHTS

SOFT-BOILED EGGS & SOLDIERS

Prep time: 5 minutes | Cook time: 16 minutes | Serves 2

- 4 large eggs
- 2 slices toast
- Butter, for spreading

1. Place your eggs into the air fryer basket.
2. Air fry the eggs at 120°C for 11 minutes.
3. When the air fryer beeps, transfer the eggs to your egg cups.
4. Cook your toast in the air fryer, then butter it and slice it widthways into soldiers about 2cm wide.
5. Serve your boiled eggs with the toast soldiers/toast sticks for dipping into the runny yolks.

SWEET POTATO HASH

Prep time: 10 minutes | Cook time: 15 minutes | Serves 4

- 1 large, sweet potato
- 1 yellow onion, finely chopped
- 1 red pepper, seeded and finely chopped
- 45ml of olive oil
- 1½ teaspoons of smoked paprika
- 1 teaspoon of sea salt
- Freshly ground pepper to taste
- 2 spring onions, thinly sliced
- Fresh chopped dill

1. Peel and chop the sweet potato into ½ cubes and place in a large bowl.
2. Preheat the air fryer to 200°C.
3. Add the onion, pepper, olive oil, paprika, salt and pepper, and toss with the potato cubes until combined.
4. Cook the mixture in batches according to the size of your air fryer.
5. Arrange the potato mixture in a single layer and cook at 200°C for 14 minutes, tossing at intervals.
6. Serve hot topped with spring onions and dill.

SAUSAGE & EGG BREAKFAST MUFFIN

Prep time: 5 minutes | **Cook time:** 20 minutes | **Serves** 2

- 4 sausages
- 1 teaspoon vegetable oil
- 2 eggs
- 2 English muffins
- 1 tablespoon butter
- 2 cheese slices
- hot sauce, to serve (optional)

1. Preheat the air fryer to 180°C for 4 minutes.
2. Remove the skins from the sausages and shape the sausage meat into 2 round patties, similar in size to the muffins. Place the patties into the air fryer and cook for 10 minutes.
3. Meanwhile, oil 2 ramekins and crack an egg into each. Cover the ramekins with some foil, making sure the foil tucks under the ramekins to hold it down. Flip the sausage patties over, then add the egg ramekins to the air fryer alongside the patties and cook for another 5 minutes.
4. Toast and butter the muffins.
5. Remove the egg ramekins and sausage patties from the air fryer. Lay 1 cheese slice on each sausage patty so the cheese gently melts in the residual heat. Carefully run a small, sharp knife around the edge of the ramekins and remove the eggs.
6. Build your muffins: place the sausage patties on the muffin bases first, followed by the eggs. Splash over hot sauce, if you like, and top with the muffin lids.

APRICOT & ALMOND PASTRIES

Prep time: 15 minutes | **Cook time:** 20 minutes | **Makes** 6

- 125 g mascarpone cheese
- 25 g icing sugar
- 50 g ground almonds
- ½ teaspoon almond extract
- 1 sheet of ready-rolled puff pastry
- beaten egg, to glaze
- 6 apricot halves, fresh or from a can, drained
- 25 g flaked almonds
- 2 tablespoons apricot jam

1. Place the mascarpone, icing sugar, ground almonds and almond extract in a bowl and mix well.
2. Unroll the puff pastry and cut it into 6 squares, about 10 cm across. Divide the almond mixture equally between the squares, spreading it out slightly but leaving a 1 cm border on all sides. Brush the edges of the pastry with a little beaten egg, then lift 2 opposite corners of one of the pastries and pinch together, before repeating with the other 2 corners, to make a parcel.
3. Push down in the centre of the parcel to make a well and pop an apricot half on top. Repeat with the remaining pastries. Brush the pastries with egg and sprinkle over the flaked almonds.
4. Cook half the pastries in a preheated air fryer at 180°C for 9–10 minutes, until risen and golden and the bases are crispy. Repeat with the remaining pastries.
5. Warm the jam, then brush over the tops of the pastries to glaze. Serve warm or cold.

MORNING DELIGHTS

STUFFED PEPPER BREAKFAST OMELETTE

Prep time: 10 minutes | **Cook time: 27 minutes** | **Serves** 2

- 4 red (bell) peppers
- 4 large eggs
- 1 tbsp whole milk
- 1 spring onion
- 125g grated Cheddar cheese
- Salt and black pepper

1. Slice the tops off the peppers and pull out the seeds. If any are left, remove them with a teaspoon, but make sure you don't make any holes in the bottoms of the peppers.
2. Place the peppers into the air fryer and cook at 180°C for 8 minutes.
3. In the meantime, crack the eggs into a mixing jug and beat well with a fork. Add the milk, season with salt and pepper and mix.
4. Finely slice the spring onion.
5. When the air fryer beeps, remove any liquid from the bottom of the peppers. Divide the cheese equally among the peppers, then pour in the egg mixture and sprinkle the spring onion on the tops.
6. Air fry the peppers at the same temperature for another 19 minutes, or until the peppers have a chargrilled look and the eggs are fully set.

MARMALADE & SEED MUFFINS

Prep time: 20 minutes | **Cook time: 15 minutes** | **Makes** 4

- 6 tablespoons thick-cut orange marmalade
- 3 tablespoons sunflower or light olive oil
- 1 egg
- 3 tablespoons milk
- 125 g plain flour
- 1 teaspoon baking powder
- ½ teaspoon ground cinnamon
- ½ teaspoon salt
- 2 tablespoons mixed seeds, such as sunflower, pumpkin and linseed
- 1 tablespoon sugar

1. Line 4 small ramekins or cake tins with paper muffin cases. In a jug, whisk 4 tablespoons of the marmalade with the oil, egg and milk.
2. Stir together the flour, baking powder, cinnamon, salt, seeds and sugar in a large bowl and stir the wet ingredients into the dry ingredients until just combined.
3. Divide the mixture equally between the cases. Cook the muffins in a preheated air fryer at 160°C for 14–15 minutes, or until a cocktail stick inserted into a muffin comes out clean.
4. Allow to cool slightly on a wire rack, then warm the remaining marmalade and spoon over the muffins. Serve warm or cold.

CHAPTER 4: MEAT LOVER'S PARADISE

MEAT LOVER'S PARADISE

STIR FRIED PORK AND LEEK

Prep time: 30 minutes | Cook time: 15 minutes | Serves 4

- 500g of pork shoulder cut into slices
- 30ml of oyster sauce
- 30ml of soy sauce
- 15ml of sesame oil
- 1 teaspoon of garlic powder
- 1 teaspoon of onion powder
- 1 teaspoon of cornflour
- ½ teaspoon of black pepper
- 130g/4.5oz of leek cleaned and sliced diagonally into ½-inch pieces

1. In a bowl, combine all the seasonings to create a marinade. Toss in the pork slices and mix well ensuring it's fully coated. Cover the bowl and marinate for at least 30 minutes.
2. Preheat the air fryer to 190°C and line with greased foil.
3. Put the marinated pork slices in the air fryer and cook for 8 minutes at 190°C, stirring once halfway through cooking.
4. Mix the leek into the air fryer with the pork and cook for a further 4–5 minutes at 190°C until the pork is cooked through.
5. Serve hot.

LAMB KOFTA WRAPS

Prep time: 5 minutes | Cook time: 15 minutes | Serves 4

- 400g minced (ground) lamb
- 1 teaspoon sumac, plus extra to finish
- 1 teaspoon za'atar
- 1 teaspoon ground coriander leaf
- ½ teaspoon cayenne pepper
- 1 tablespoon ground cumin
- finely grated zest of 1 lemon
- 2 tablespoons roughly chopped flat-leaf parsley leaves
- 4 flatbreads
- 150g hummus
- 2 Little Gem lettuces
- 4 tablespoons pomegranate seeds
- salt and pepper
- Extra-virgin olive oil, to serve

1. Preheat the air fryer to 170°C for 4 minutes.
2. In a medium-sized bowl, mix together the lamb and all the dried herbs and spices, then season well with salt. Add the lemon zest and parsley. Form into small kofta shapes, around 50g each. Place into the air fryer and cook for 6 minutes until cooked through.
3. Meanwhile, heat a frying pan over a medium heat. Once hot, heat the flatbreads for around 15 seconds on each side.
4. To serve, spread the hummus over the flatbreads, then top with the lettuce and koftas, sprinkle over the pomegranate seeds. Finish with a drizzle of oil and a grind of pepper.

CHAPTER 4

PORK & APPLE BURGERS

Prep time: 5 minutes | **Cook time:** 10 minutes | **Serves** 4

- 350 g minced/ground pork
- 1 teaspoon grated root ginger
- 1 eating apple, grated (peel on is fine)
- 2 tablespoons breadcrumbs
- ½ teaspoon dried thyme
- ¾ teaspoon salt
- ¼ teaspoon freshly ground black pepper
- 1 teaspoon olive oil, either in a spray bottle or simply to drizzle over

1. Mix all the ingredients except the olive oil together and mould into 4 equal-sized burgers. Place on a sheet of baking paper. Spray the burgers with olive oil or drizzle it over if you don't have a spray bottle.
2. Preheat the air fryer to 180°C. Add the burgers on the paper to the preheated air fryer and cook for 8 minutes on one side, then carefully turn and cook for 7 minutes on the other side. Check the internal temperature of the thickest part has reached 71°C on a food thermometer; if not, cook for a few more minutes before serving.

BACON AND BROCCOLI QUICHE CUPS

Prep time: 10 minutes | **Cook time:** 30 minutes | **Serves** 2

- 4 bacon strips, chopped
- 25g of broccoli, broken into small florets
- 25g of chopped onion
- 1 garlic clove, finely chopped
- 3 eggs
- 25g of dried parsley flakes
- Salt and pepper to taste
- 115g shredded Cheddar cheese
- 30g of chopped tomato

1. Fry the chopped bacon in a pan until crispy. Transfer to paper towels to soak up the liquid and keep what is in the frying pan to use again.
2. Using the same pan and the liquid from the bacon, add the broccoli and onion to and cook for 2-3 minutes until tender. Add the garlic and cook for a further minute.
3. Whisk the eggs, parsley, salt, and pepper in a separate bowl until thoroughly combined. Add the cheese, tomato, bacon, and broccoli mixture, and stir.
4. Preheat the air fryer to 200°C.
5. Pour the quiche mixture evenly between 2 greased 280ml ramekins, and place in the air fryer.
6. Cook at 200°C for 20-25 minutes or until a knife inserted in the centre comes out clean.
7. Serve hot or cold.

MEAT LOVER'S PARADISE

TONNATO STEAK

Prep time: 5 minutes | **Cook time:** 25 minutes | **Serves** 2

- 1 × 3cm thick sirloin steak, about 400g
- 1 tablespoon extra-virgin olive oil
- 40g rocket (arugula)
- 200g cherry tomatoes, halved
- 2 tablespoons crispy shallots
- salt and pepper

For The Dressing

- 150g can tuna, drained (112g drained weight)
- 3 anchovy fillets
- ½ garlic clove
- 2 egg yolks
- 85ml extra-virgin olive oil
- 1 tablespoon white wine vinegar
- juice of ½ lemon
- 1 tablespoon capers

1. Take the steak out of the fridge at least 30 minutes before cooking. Preheat the air fryer to 200°C for 4 minutes.
2. Rub both sides of the steak with the olive oil, then add a generous sprinkle of salt and pepper to both sides. Put the steak into the air fryer and cook for 8 minutes, turning over halfway through. Once ready, rest the steak for 5–10 minutes. This timing should give you the perfect medium-rare steak.
3. Meanwhile, prepare the dressing. Put the tuna, anchovy, garlic and egg yolks into a blender. Blitz, gradually drizzling in the olive oil, until emulsified. Stir in the vinegar, lemon juice and capers. The sauce should be thick, but you should still be able to easily drizzle it. If it is looking too thick, just add a splash of water.
4. To serve, scatter the rocket on a platter, then top with the sliced steak, tomatoes, dressing and crispy shallots.

FRUITY PORK STEAKS

Prep time: 10 minutes | **Cook time:** 15 minutes | **Serves** 2

- 2 red apples
- 2 pears
- Extra-virgin olive oil spray
- 1 tsp ground cinnamon
- 2 x 225g/8oz pork steaks
- 2 tsp pork or poultry seasoning
- Salt and black pepper

1. Leaving the skins on, dice the apples and pears. Place them into the air fryer basket, spreading them out. Spray with olive oil and sprinkle with cinnamon.
2. Place the pork steaks over the fruit and sprinkle half the pork seasoning over them. Season generously with salt and pepper.
3. Air fry at 180°C for 8 minutes. Turn the pork steaks over and sprinkle with the remaining pork seasoning, along with extra salt and pepper.
4. Air fry at the same temperature for a final 6 minutes, or until the pork steaks are firm and the fruit is fork tender.

SPICED PORK FILLETS

Prep time: 10 minutes | **Cook time:** 20 minutes | **Serves** 8

- 900g of pork tenderloin steak
- 30ml of olive oil
- 3 garlic cloves, finely chopped
- 30g of brown sugar
- 2 teaspoons of chilli powder
- 2 teaspoons of ground cumin
- 2 teaspoons of onion powder
- 1 teaspoon of thyme
- Salt and pepper to taste

1. Remove the tenderloin from any packaging and pat dry with kitchen roll.
2. Slip the point of a knife under the silver skin of the pork and gently cut and pull to remove it.
3. Put all the dry ingredients in a bowl and mix thoroughly.
4. Pour in the olive oil, add the garlic and mix again until combined.
5. Rub the seasoning mixture all over the pork.
6. Preheat the air fryer to 200°C.
7. Put the seasoned pork tenderloin into the air fryer. Cook for 16–17 minutes at 200°C.
8. Remove the pork from the air fryer and allow to rest for a few minutes before serving.

MEAT LOVER'S PARADISE

SHEPHERD'S PIE

Prep time: 20 minutes | **Cook time:** 30 minutes | **Serves** 4

- 500g lamb mince
- 1 onion, finely chopped
- 2 carrots, diced
- 1 tablespoon tomato purée
- 1 tablespoon plain flour
- 300ml beef stock
- 1 tablespoon Worcestershire sauce
- 1 teaspoon fresh thyme (or ½ teaspoon dried thyme)
- Salt and pepper, to taste
- 800g Maris Piper potatoes, peeled and chopped
- 50g butter
- 100ml whole milk
- 100g cheddar cheese, grated (optional)

1. Preheat your air fryer to 200°C.
2. Cook the lamb mixture: In a large pan, cook the lamb mince over medium heat until browned, breaking it up with a wooden spoon. Drain off any excess fat. Add the chopped onion and carrots to the pan and cook for another 5 minutes until softened. Stir in the tomato purée and flour, cooking for 1 minute. Gradually pour in the beef stock, stirring constantly. Add the Worcestershire sauce, thyme, salt, and pepper. Simmer for 15 minutes until the sauce has thickened.
3. Make the mashed potatoes: Boil the potatoes in a large pot of salted water for 10-12 minutes until tender. Drain and mash with the butter and milk. Season with salt and pepper.
4. Assemble the shepherd's pie: Transfer the lamb mixture to an ovenproof dish. Spoon the mashed potato over the top, spreading it evenly. If you like, sprinkle grated cheddar cheese on top.
5. Cook in the air fryer: Place the shepherd's pie in the air fryer basket and cook for 25-30 minutes, or until the top is golden and crisp.
6. Let it cool slightly before serving.

25

CHAPTER 4

BACON AND TURKEY BURGER BITES

Prep time: 10 minutes | **Cook time:** 20 minutes | **Serves** 15

- 900g minced turkey
- 120g centre cut raw bacon, minced
- 30g yellow mustard
- ½ teaspoon of onion powder
- Salt to taste
- Pepper to taste
- 1 head of butter lettuce
- 30 cherry tomatoes
- 2–3 jalapeño sliced in 30 thin slices, optional
- 30 dill pickle chips or slices
- Ketchup, mayo and/or yellow mustard, optional for dipping

1. In a bowl, use your hands to mix the turkey, bacon, mustard, salt, onion powder and pepper.
2. Use a tablespoon to scoop out the mixture to create 30 burger bites about the size of a golf ball.
3. Preheat the air fryer to 200°C.
4. Arrange the burger bites in a single layer in the air fryer. Cook in batches if they will not all fit.
5. Cook at 200°C for about 8 to 10 minutes turning about halfway through cooking. Cook for longer if you prefer the meat well-done.
6. Skewer the burger bites with salad vegetables and pickles and serve with a selection of dipping sauces.

COUNTRY FRIED PORK CHOPS

Prep time: 10 minutes | **Cook time:** 15 minutes | **Serves** 4

- 4 pork loin chops
- 1 teaspoon sea salt
- 1 teaspoon freshly ground black pepper
- 100g Italian-seasoned Breadcrumbs
- 1 tablespoon garlic powder
- 120g plain flour
- 1 large egg, beaten
- Olive oil cooking spray

1. Rinse the pork chops and pat dry with paper towels. Sprinkle with the salt and pepper.
2. In a shallow bowl, combine the breadcrumbs and garlic powder. Dip each pork chop into the flour, then the beaten egg, then dredge in the breadcrumb mixture, turning to coat evenly.
3. Spray on all sides with olive oil and place in the basket.
4. Air fry in batches at 210°C for 10 minutes, then flip chops and continue to air fry until cooked through and golden, about 5 minutes.

CHAPTER 5: CHICKEN AND FISH DISHES

CHAPTER 5

BEETROOT SIDE OF SALMON

Prep time: 5 minutes | **Cook time:** 45 minutes | **Serves** 2

- 250g raw beetroot, cut into 4cm cubes
- 3 garlic cloves, bashed but kept in their skins
- 2 tablespoons extra-virgin olive oil
- 200g Tenderstem® broccoli
- 500g side of salmon
- 2 tablespoons strained Greek yogurt
- 1 tablespoon sherry vinegar
- ½ teaspoon sumac
- Salt and black pepper
- Rye bread, to serve (optional)

1. Preheat the air fryer to 170°C for 4 minutes.
2. Put the beetroot and garlic on a piece of foil in the air fryer basket, then drizzle over 1 tablespoon of the oil and cook for 20 minutes. Remove the garlic, increase the temperature to 180°C and cook the beetroot for a further 10 minutes until tender. Remove and set aside. Reduce the air fryer temperature to 170°C.
3. Place the broccoli in the section underneath the air fryer basket if you have one (otherwise place in the basket), and drizzle with the remaining 1 tablespoon of oil.
4. Put the salmon on a piece of foil or baking parchment and place in the air fryer basket. Cook for 10 minutes until the flesh of the salmon is firm and coral pink in colour, and the broccoli is tender.
5. Meanwhile, squeeze the garlic cloves out of their skins and add to a blender along with the beetroot, Greek yogurt, sherry vinegar and some salt. Blitz and set aside.
6. Serve the salmon with the broccoli and the beetroot sauce and sprinkle over the sumac and a grind of black pepper. Offer rye bread on the side, if you like.

LONDON FRIED FISH

Prep time: 10 minutes | **Cook time:** 15 minutes | **Serves** 4

- 450g sole fillets
- 75g plain flour
- 2 large eggs, beaten
- 100g fresh breadcrumbs
- 1 teaspoon sea salt
- 1 teaspoon freshly ground black pepper
- Olive oil cooking spray

1. Slice the sole fillets lengthwise into 2.5cm wide strips.
2. Dredge each strip in the flour, coating on each side. Dip into the beaten egg, then press each side into the breadcrumbs, coating evenly.
3. Preheat the air fryer to 200°C.
4. Place the fish strips into the air fryer, leaving space between each one. Sprinkle with salt and pepper. Spray with cooking spray.
5. Cook for 12-15 minutes until golden brown and cooked through. The fish should flake easily when tested with a fork.

CHICKEN AND FISH DISHES

SUPER-CRISPY CHICKEN SCHNITZEL

Prep time: 10 minutes | **Cook time:** 15 minutes | **Serves** 2

- 2 medium chicken breast fillets
- 2 teaspoons dried mixed herbs
- 100g plain flour
- 1 tablespoon dried parsley
- 2 large eggs
- ½ teaspoon garlic powder
- 100g fresh breadcrumbs
- 1 tablespoon dried poultry seasoning
- Salt and black pepper

1. Start by butterflying the chicken breast fillets to flatten them out. Place a breast on a chopping board and position a sharp knife at the side. Slice horizontally, cutting about three quarters of the way through, then open the chicken out like a book. Repeat to butterfly the second chicken breast fillet.
2. Generously season the chicken with the mixed herbs and salt and pepper. Place on a large plate, cover and place in the fridge for an hour.
3. Create a production line: put the flour, parsley and salt and pepper in the first bowl. In the second bowl, combine the eggs and garlic powder, and season with salt and pepper. Beat with a fork. In the third and final bowl, mix the breadcrumbs with the dried poultry seasoning and season generously with salt and pepper.
4. To coat the butterflied chicken breast fillets, dip them first in the flour bowl, turning to coat, then drench in egg and let the excess drip off. Finally, roll in the breadcrumbs until each piece is fully covered in crumbs.
5. Place the chicken schnitzel into the air fryer basket, making sure they are not touching one another. If your air fryer is small, you might need to cook them in two batches. Air fry at 180°C for 12 minutes, or until a thermometer reads 75°C in the thickest part and they are golden and crispy.

CHAPTER 5

TUNA PASTA BAKE

Prep time: 5 minutes | **Cook time:** 10 minutes | **Serves** 2

- 300g leftover cooked pasta (penne or macaroni)
- 250g passata
- 200g chopped tomatoes (½ standard tin)
- 35g cream cheese
- 145g tinned tuna, drained
- ½ teaspoon runny honey
- ½ teaspoon dried chilli flakes
- 30g fresh basil leaves, chopped, plus extra to garnish (or 1 teaspoon dried)
- 50g Cheddar, grated
- ½ teaspoon salt
- ¼ teaspoon freshly ground black pepper
- 50g mozzarella, torn or grated

1. Mix all ingredients except the mozzarella in a bowl. Turn the mixture out into a heatproof dish that fits in your air fryer and top with the mozzarella. Place the dish in the air fryer.
2. Set the air fryer to 170°C and cook for 15-16 minutes (no need to preheat the air fryer).
3. Serve immediately, garnished with a few extra basil leaves.

FISH PIE

Prep time: 5 minutes | **Cook time:** 20 minutes | **Serves** 2

- 450g frozen fish pie mix, defrosted overnight
- 300ml water, or enough to cover the fish
- 75g frozen spinach, defrosted and squeezed
- 75g frozen peas
- 50g frozen sweetcorn
- ¼ teaspoon mustard powder
- 1 teaspoon salt
- ½ teaspoon freshly ground black pepper
- 1 tablespoon fresh or frozen chopped parsley
- 200g crème fraîche
- 400g leftover mashed potatoes, warmed
- 15g butter, melted

1. Place the defrosted fish pie mix in a saucepan, cover with water and bring to simmer. As soon as fish is opaque, remove the pan from the heat and drain. Add the spinach, peas, sweetcorn, mustard powder, salt, pepper, parsley and crème fraîche to the saucepan. Stir to mix with the fish and heat over a low-medium heat for 3-4 minutes.
2. Place this mixture in the bottom of a heatproof pie dish that fits in your air fryer. Top with warmed mashed potato – it doesn't have to be hot, but it does need to be malleable so that you can cover the top of the pie. You can either pipe the potato on top or push it down with a fork, then brush the top with the melted butter.
3. Place the pie dish in the air fryer. Set the air fryer to 160°C and cook for 12 minutes (no need to preheat the air fryer). Remove from the air fryer and serve with your choice of vegetables.

CHICKEN AND FISH DISHES

CHICKEN MASSAMAN CURRY

Prep time: 5 minutes | **Cook time:** 20 minutes | **Serves** 2

- 50g frozen green beans
- 80g frozen spinach
- 200ml coconut milk (from a tin or carton)
- 200ml hot vegetable stock
- 30g massaman curry paste
- 1 teaspoon fish sauce
- 1½ tablespoons smooth peanut butter
- 1 tablespoon brown sugar
- 100g leftover cooked chicken, roughly torn or sliced
- 50g frozen peas
- Fresh basil leaves (optional)
- Cooked rice, to serve

1. Place the frozen beans and spinach in a heatproof dish that fits in your air fryer. Mix together the coconut milk, hot stock, curry paste, fish sauce, peanut butter and brown sugar in a bowl and pour this over the vegetables.
2. Preheat the air fryer to 160°C. Place the dish in the preheated air fryer and cook for 8 minutes, then stir in the chicken and frozen peas and cook for a further 10 minutes.
3. Serve with cooked rice and scatter over fresh basil, if using.

A WHOLE CHICKEN

Prep time: 5 minutes | **Cook time:** 45 minutes | **Serves** 4

- 1 medium whole chicken (giblets removed)
- ½ tbsp extra-virgin olive oil
- 1½ tsp dried mixed herbs/Italian seasoning
- Salt and black pepper

1. Tie the chicken legs together with kitchen string.
2. Place the whole chicken, breast side down, on a chopping board. Rub half the olive oil into all the visible skin, then sprinkle half the mixed herbs over the chicken and season with salt and pepper.
3. Place the chicken into the air fryer basket, still breast side down, and air fry at 180°C for 25 minutes.
4. Place a fork in the cavity and use it to flip the chicken over so that it is breast side up. Drizzle with the remaining olive oil and rub into the skin, then add the remaining herbs and extra salt and pepper.
5. Cook at the same temperature for a further 20 minutes, or until a thermometer reads an internal temperature of 75°C in the thickest part of the thigh.

CHAPTER 5

PINEAPPLE & PIRI PIRI TURKEY BURGERS

Prep time: 10 minutes | **Cook time:** 20 minutes | **Serves** 4

For the burgers:
- 500g minced turkey
- 1 bunch spring onions, finely chopped
- 2 tablespoons piri piri seasoning
- 1 lemon, finely grated zest and juice
- Salt and pepper

To serve:
- 4 brioche burger buns, halved
- Sunflower oil spray
- 4 tinned pineapple rings, drained
- 4 tablespoons light mayonnaise
- 2 tablespoons piri piri sauce
- 4 round lettuce leaves
- 8 red onion rings

1. Place all the burger ingredients in a large bowl and mix until well combined. Shape the mixture into 4 burgers.
2. Preheat the air fryer to 200°C. Arrange the burger buns, cut sides down, and cook for 1-2 minutes, until lightly toasted, then remove. You may need to do this in 2 batches.
3. Place the burgers in the air fryer, spritz with oil and cook at 180°C for 14-16 minutes, turning halfway through, until the internal temperature reaches 75°C.
4. Remove the burgers, increase the temperature to 200°C and cook the pineapple rings for 2-3 minutes, turning once, until starting to caramelise.
5. Mix the mayonnaise with the piri piri sauce and spread over the bun bases. Top each with a lettuce leaf, burger, pineapple ring and 2 slices of onion. Add the lids and serve immediately.

CHICKEN AND FISH DISHES

TURKEY SATAY

Prep time: 5 minutes | Cook time: 20 minutes | Serves 2

For the turkey:

- 1 teaspoon paprika
- 1 teaspoon ground turmeric
- 2 tablespoons olive oil
- 550g turkey breast, cut into strips or cubes
- Salt and freshly ground black pepper
- Lime wedges, to serve
- Wooden skewers to fit your air fryer

For the satay dip:

- 200ml coconut milk
- 3 tablespoons smooth peanut butter
- 1 teaspoon soy sauce
- 1 teaspoon Thai curry paste
- ½ teaspoon runny honey

1. Mix the paprika and turmeric with the oil in a bowl, then add turkey and stir to coat the pieces. Thread the coated pieces onto skewers.
2. Preheat the air fryer to 180°C. Place the skewers in the preheated air fryer and cook for 7-8 minutes, turning once. Check the internal temperature of the turkey has reached 75°C using a food thermometer inserted into the thickest part – if it hasn't, cook for a few more minutes.
3. Place all the satay dip ingredients in a heatproof bowl that fits in your air fryer and stir well. Preheat the air fryer to 190°C. Add the bowl to the preheated air fryer and cook for 3-5 minutes, stirring twice during cooking.
4. Serve the warm dip with the turkey skewers and lime wedges for squeezing over.

BEER-BATTERED FISH AND CHIPS

Prep time: 15 minutes | Cook time: 25 minutes | Serves 2

- 300g cod fillets (or haddock)
- 100g plain flour, plus extra for dusting
- 150ml cold beer (lager or ale)
- ½ teaspoon baking powder
- 2 large Maris Piper potatoes (about 400g)
- 2 tablespoons sunflower oil
- Salt and malt vinegar, for serving
- Optional: mushy peas, to serve

1. Preheat your air fryer to 200°C.
2. Peel the potatoes and cut into chips about 1cm thick. Toss with 1 tablespoon of the oil and season with salt.
3. Place the chips in the air fryer basket and cook for 12 minutes, shaking halfway through.
4. Meanwhile, mix the flour, baking powder, and a pinch of salt in a large bowl. Whisk in the cold beer until you have a smooth, thick batter.
5. Pat the fish dry and dust lightly with flour. Dip each fillet into the batter, ensuring it is fully coated.
6. Remove the chips and keep warm. Place the battered fish fillets in the air fryer basket, making sure they are not touching. Spray or brush with remaining oil and cook for 6-7 minutes per side, or until golden brown and cooked through (the fish should flake easily).
7. Return the chips to the air fryer for a final 3-4 minutes to crisp up.
8. Serve the fish and chips with salt, malt vinegar, and mushy peas if desired.

CHAPTER 6: VEGETABLE-BASED CREATIONS

VEGETABLE-BASED CREATIONS

CRISPY BUTTERNUT SQUASH GNOCCHI

Prep time: 5 minutes | **Cook time:** 22 minutes | **Serves** 2

- 250g butternut squash, peeled, deseeded and cut into 2.5cm cubes
- 1 tablespoon olive oil
- 250g vegan gnocchi
- 1 small red onion, cut into wedges
- 8 fresh sage leaves
- 50g baby spinach
- 2 tablespoons vegan pesto
- 1 tablespoon pine nuts, toasted
- Salt and freshly ground black pepper

1. Place the butternut squash in a bowl and toss with 1 teaspoon of the oil. Season with salt and pepper. Cook in a preheated air fryer at 200°C for 10 minutes, shaking the basket halfway through.
2. Toss the gnocchi, onion wedges and sage leaves in the remaining oil, add to the air fryer and cook for a further 10-12 minutes, shaking the basket a couple of times, until the gnocchi is crispy and the squash is tender. Add the spinach about 1 minute before the end of the cooking time. Stir well until the spinach has wilted.
3. Transfer to 2 serving plates, drizzle with the pesto and finish with a good grinding of black pepper and the toasted pine nuts. Serve immediately.

POTATO CAKES

Prep time: 5 minutes | **Cook time:** 20 minutes | **Serves** 2

- 450g mashed potato (or the flesh of leftover baked potatoes)
- 3 spring onions, finely sliced
- 1 teaspoon smoked paprika
- 1 teaspoon garlic salt
- ⅛ teaspoon freshly ground black pepper
- 1 teaspoon dried oregano
- 80g mature Cheddar, grated
- 1 large egg, beaten
- 1-2 tablespoons plain flour
- ½ teaspoon olive oil, for drizzling

1. In a large bowl, combine the mashed potato with the sliced spring onions, spices, oregano and grated cheese. Stir together, then add the beaten egg. Add enough flour to bind the mixture – you may need up to 2 tablespoons depending on how wet your potatoes are. Mix thoroughly. Shape into 6 flat cakes, each roughly the size of a burger. Drizzle the top of each with olive oil.
2. Preheat the air fryer to 190°C. Place the potato cakes in the preheated air fryer (you may need to cook them in batches, depending on the size of your air fryer) and cook for 15 minutes, turning after 10 minutes, until crispy on the outside.

35

CHAPTER 6

MUSHROOM BURGERS & TRADITIONAL COLESLAW

Prep time: 15 minutes | **Cook time:** 15 minutes | **Serves** 4

- **For the burgers:**
- 4 large Portobello mushrooms
- 4 burger buns, halved and toasted
- 2 tablespoons soy sauce
- 1 tablespoon honey
- 1 garlic clove, crushed
- 1 teaspoon grated ginger
- Sesame seeds
- **For the coleslaw:**
- ½ head of red cabbage, shredded
- 2 carrots, grated
- ¼ cup mayonnaise
- 1 tablespoon apple apple cider vinegar
- 1 teaspoon sugar
- Salt and pepper to taste

1. In a small bowl, whisk together soy sauce, honey, garlic and ginger.
2. Brush the marinade onto both sides of the mushrooms. Sprinkle with sesame seeds.
3. Preheat your air fryer to 200°C. Place the mushrooms in the air fryer basket and cook for 7-10 minutes per side, or until tender and lightly charred.
4. Meanwhile, make the coleslaw by combining the shredded cabbage, grated carrots, mayonnaise, cider vinegar, sugar, salt and pepper. Toss well to combine.
5. Assemble the burgers by placing a mushroom on each toasted bun base. Top with coleslaw and the bun lid. Serve immediately.

MEDITERRANEAN-STYLE AIR-FRIED VEGETABLES

Prep time: 30 minutes | **Cook time:** 30 minutes | **Serves** 4

- 1 aubergine
- 1 courgette (try using ½ green and ½ yellow for colour)
- 250g button mushrooms
- 1 green pepper
- 1 red pepper
- 2 garlic cloves, peeled and finely chopped
- 100ml white wine
- 15ml vegetable oil
- Salt and freshly ground black pepper

1. Cut the aubergine into 1cm-thick semi-circular slices and sprinkle with salt. Leave for 30 minutes to draw out excess moisture.
2. Meanwhile, slice the courgette into thin rounds.
3. Halve the mushrooms.
4. Remove the seeds from the peppers and slice into thin strips.
5. Peel and finely chop the garlic.
6. Preheat the air fryer to 180°C.
7. Rinse the salt off the aubergine and pat dry with kitchen paper. Place in the bottom of the air fryer basket with the chopped garlic.
8. Add the remaining vegetables and pour over the wine and oil.
9. Cook for 20-30 minutes at 180°C, until the vegetables are tender.
10. Serve immediately with steamed white or brown rice.

VEGETABLE-BASED CREATIONS

SPICED CAULIFLOWER STEAKS

Prep time: 5 minutes | Cook time: 15 minutes | Serves 2

- 1 tablespoon olive oil
- 2 cauliflower steaks (2.5cm thick), cut from the centre of the cauliflower
- ½ teaspoon ground turmeric
- ½ teaspoon garlic powder
- ½ teaspoon nigella seeds
- Salt and freshly ground black pepper
- Fresh tomatoes, chopped
- Red onion, thinly sliced
- Fresh mint leaves, to serve

1. In a small bowl, mix the oil, turmeric, garlic powder and a good pinch of salt. Brush this mixture over the cauliflower steaks. Preheat the air fryer to 180°C.
2. Place the cauliflower steaks in the preheated air fryer and cook for 8 minutes on one side, then turn over and cook for a further 7 minutes until tender and lightly charred.
3. Serve scattered with nigella seeds, a drizzle of olive oil and the chopped tomatoes, sliced onion and mint leaves.

CREAMY MUSHROOM STROGANOFF

Prep time: 10 minutes | Cook time: 15 minutes | Serves 2

- 225g button mushrooms
- 1 large onion
- 1 tablespoon smoked paprika
- 340g soft cheese
- 120ml vegetable stock
- 1 teaspoon garlic purée
- 1 teaspoon dried parsley
- Salt and freshly ground black pepper
- Cooked pasta, to serve

1. Halve the mushrooms and peel and slice the onion lengthways. Place in the air fryer, sprinkle with 1 teaspoon of the paprika, and season with salt and pepper.
2. Air fry at 180°C for 8 minutes, then transfer the mushrooms and onions to a silicone-lined baking tin.
3. Add the soft cheese, remaining paprika, vegetable stock, garlic purée and parsley to the tin. Season generously with salt and pepper, stir well and place back into the air fryer basket. Cook at the same temperature for 6 minutes, or until you have a hot, creamy sauce. Serve over freshly cooked pasta.

CHAPTER 6

RAINBOW BRUNCH BOWL

Prep time: 10 minutes | **Cook time:** 25 minutes | **Serves** 2

- 1 medium courgette
- 1 red pepper
- 225g sweet potato, peeled and diced
- 225g butternut squash, peeled and diced
- 2 teaspoons dried parsley
- 2 teaspoons mixed herbs
- 2 teaspoons sweet paprika
- 1 tablespoon extra virgin olive oil
- 5 Cumberland sausages
- Salt and freshly ground black pepper

1. Cut the courgette into thick slices, then quarter each slice. Remove the seeds from the pepper and dice. Place in a bowl with the sweet potato and butternut squash cubes.
2. Add the dried herbs, paprika and olive oil, then season with salt and pepper and mix well with your hands.
3. Transfer the vegetables to the air fryer basket and cook at 160°C for 12 minutes. Stir with a silicone spatula, then cut your sausages into quarters and arrange over the vegetables.
4. Increase the temperature to 180°C and cook for a further 8 minutes, then stir the sausages into the vegetables. Finally, increase to 200°C and cook for 5 minutes more, or until the sausages are well browned.
5. Divide between two bowls and serve hot.

COURGETTE AND FETA BALLS

Prep time: 10 minutes | **Cook time:** 10 minutes | **Serves** 4

- 170g porridge oats
- 150g courgette
- 45g feta cheese
- 1 large egg, beaten
- Finely grated zest of 1 lemon
- 6 fresh basil leaves, finely sliced
- 1 teaspoon fresh dill, chopped
- 1 teaspoon dried oregano
- Salt and freshly ground black pepper

1. Coarsely grate the courgette and squeeze out any excess moisture using a clean tea towel.
2. Mix the egg and courgette together in a bowl. Crumble in the feta and add the seasonings, setting aside the oats.
3. Blitz the oats in a food processor until they resemble fine breadcrumbs. Gradually fold into the courgette mixture – the mixture will thicken quickly.
4. Preheat your air fryer to 200°C. Line with foil or baking parchment.
5. Shape the mixture into balls and arrange in the air fryer basket in a single layer, leaving space between each one.
6. Cook for 10 minutes at 200°C until golden brown.
7. Serve hot with spaghetti.

38

VEGETABLE-BASED CREATIONS

TERIYAKI VEGETABLES

Prep time: 10 minutes | Cook time: 20 minutes | Serves 4

- 1 small head of broccoli, cut into florets
- 4 chestnut mushrooms
- 1 pepper, any colour
- 1 medium courgette
- 15ml olive oil
- 2 teaspoons Chinese five-spice
- Salt and freshly ground black pepper
- 45ml teriyaki sauce

1. Cut all the vegetables into similar-sized pieces and toss in a bowl with the Chinese five-spice, salt and pepper.
2. Preheat the air fryer to 180°C.
3. Add the olive oil to the bowl of vegetables and mix well to coat.
4. Transfer to the air fryer and cook for 14 minutes at 180°C.
5. Return the vegetables to the bowl and stir in the teriyaki sauce.
6. Line the air fryer basket with foil and return the vegetables to the basket.
7. Cook for a further 5 minutes at 180°C.
8. Serve hot with steamed rice.

SUMMER VEGETABLE GRATIN

Prep time: 10 minutes | Cook time: 55 minutes | Serves 4

- 1 medium courgette
- 1 medium yellow squash
- 1 small aubergine, peeled
- 1 tablespoon salt
- 2 tablespoons olive oil
- 50g mature Cheddar, grated
- 50g seasoned breadcrumbs
- 1 garlic clove, finely chopped
- ½ teaspoon freshly ground black pepper
- 25g Parmesan cheese, freshly grated
- Olive oil cooking spray
- 2 tablespoons fresh flat-leaf parsley, chopped

1. Coarsely grate the courgette, yellow squash and aubergine. Toss with the salt and leave in a colander to drain for at least 30 minutes and up to 90 minutes. Rinse with cool water to remove excess salt, then squeeze dry in a clean tea towel. Toss with the olive oil and grated Cheddar.
2. In a small bowl, combine the breadcrumbs, garlic, pepper and Parmesan cheese.
3. Lightly coat the air fryer pan with olive oil spray, then add the vegetable mixture. Top with the breadcrumb mixture.
4. Cook at 175°C until the vegetables are tender, about 25 minutes. Scatter over the parsley before serving.

CHAPTER 7: TASTY SIDES AND SNACKS

TASTY SIDES AND SNACKS

CHEESE-STUFFED PORTOBELLO MUSHROOMS

Prep time: 10 minutes | **Cook time:** 13 minutes | **Serves** 4

- 1 tablespoon extra virgin olive oil
- 8 large Portobello mushroom caps, stems and gills removed
- 100g Münster cheese, grated
- 100g mature Cheddar cheese, grated
- 100g plain flour
- 2 large eggs, beaten
- 100g panko breadcrumbs
- Olive oil cooking spray

1. Heat the olive oil in a large frying pan over medium-high heat. Add the mushroom caps and sear on each side for 4-5 minutes. Remove from pan and pat dry with kitchen paper to remove excess moisture.
2. Fill one mushroom cap with a quarter of both cheeses, then top with another cap. Repeat with remaining mushrooms and cheese.
3. Coat each mushroom stack first in flour, then dip in beaten egg, and finally coat in breadcrumbs. Spray lightly with olive oil.
4. Place 1-2 mushroom stacks in the air fryer. Cook at 195°C for about 6 minutes, turning halfway through, until the cheese has melted. Repeat with remaining stacks.

PARMESAN CHICKEN WINGS

Prep time: 5 minutes | **Cook time:** 20 minutes | **Serves** 2

- 1 tablespoon baking powder
- 1 teaspoon garlic powder
- 1 tablespoon dried oregano
- 400g chicken wings, wing tips removed and jointed
- 30g unsalted butter
- 1 garlic clove, finely grated
- 20g Parmesan cheese, finely grated, plus extra for serving
- Finely grated zest of 1 lemon
- 5g fresh chives, finely chopped
- Olive oil or vegetable oil, for spraying
- Salt and freshly ground black pepper

1. Preheat the air fryer to 200°C for 4 minutes.
2. In a medium bowl, mix together the baking powder, garlic powder, oregano and a pinch of salt. Add the wings and toss to coat. Arrange the wings in the air fryer basket skin-side up in a single layer. Spray generously with oil and cook for about 15 minutes until crispy and golden.
3. Meanwhile, melt the butter with the grated garlic in a small bowl in the microwave for 40 seconds. Transfer to a medium bowl and stir in the Parmesan and lemon zest. When the wings are ready, toss them in the Parmesan mixture.
4. Serve garnished with chives, extra Parmesan and freshly ground black pepper.

CHAPTER 7

CRISPY POTATO WEDGES

Prep time: 10 minutes | Cook time: 30 minutes | Serves 4

- 4 large Maris Piper potatoes
- 2 tbsp olive oil
- 1 tsp paprika
- 1 tsp garlic powder
- ½ tsp dried thyme
- ½ tsp dried oregano
- Sea salt, to taste
- Freshly ground black pepper, to taste

1. Scrub the potatoes clean but leave the skins on. Cut each potato into wedges – first in half, then slice each half into 3 or 4 wedges depending on size.
2. In a large bowl, toss the wedges with the olive oil, paprika, garlic powder, thyme, oregano, sea salt, and black pepper until evenly coated.
3. Preheat the air fryer to 200°C.
4. Place the potato wedges in the air fryer basket in a single layer. If they don't all fit, cook them in batches to avoid overcrowding.
5. Air fry for 20-25 minutes, shaking the basket halfway through cooking to ensure even crisping. The wedges should be golden brown and crispy when done.
6. Once cooked, remove from the air fryer and sprinkle with a little extra sea salt, if desired.

CHOCOLATE VELVET CAKE

Prep time: 10 minutes | Cook time: 30 minutes | Serves 2

- 175g plain flour
- 150g caster sugar
- 3 tablespoons cocoa powder
- 1 teaspoon bicarbonate of soda
- ½ teaspoon sea salt
- 1 teaspoon vanilla extract
- 60ml vegetable oil
- 100ml water
- 1 tablespoon white wine vinegar
- Vegetable oil cooking spray

1. In a large bowl, combine all ingredients except the cooking spray using an electric hand whisk until just combined.
2. Lightly grease the air fryer pan with cooking spray and pour in the cake mixture.
3. Cook at 165°C for about 30 minutes, or until a skewer inserted into the middle comes out clean.
4. Remove from the air fryer and leave to cool for 30 minutes before serving.

TASTY SIDES AND SNACKS

PERFECT POTATO PANCAKES

Prep time: 10 minutes | Cook time: 30 minutes | Serves 4

- 2 medium or large russet potatoes, peeled
- 1 small onion
- 1 large egg, beaten
- 1 teaspoon sea salt
- ½ teaspoon freshly ground pepper
- 3 tablespoons plain flour

1. Put the potatoes in a pot and cover with water. Bring to a boil, and cook potatoes until you can just sink a fork into them—they should still be firm—about 10 minutes. Drain and let them cool enough to handle. Using a box grater, grate the onion and potatoes and toss together to combine. Place the grated mixture in a tight mesh strainer and press to release excess liquid. Blot the mixture with a paper towel and place in a large bowl.
2. Add the egg, salt, and pepper and stir with a fork to mix. Next, add the flour 1 tablespoon at a time, mixing thoroughly between each addition.
3. Scoop about ¼ of the mixture into the palm of your hand and form it into a patty. Repeat with remaining mixture. Place 1 patty at a time in the air fryer basket.
4. Air fry in batches at 210°C until golden brown, about 20 minutes.

SWEET, SALT, OR BUTTER POPCORN

Prep time: 10 minutes | Cook time: 15 minutes | Serves 4

- 75g popping corn
- ½ teaspoon olive oil

Optional toppings:

- ½ teaspoon salt
- 1 teaspoon caster sugar
- 1 tablespoon melted butter

1. Preheat the air fryer to 200°C.
2. In a bowl, toss the popping corn with the olive oil until well coated.
3. Spread the kernels evenly across the base of the air fryer pan, ensuring they're not too tightly packed.
4. Close the air fryer securely to contain the popping kernels.
5. Cook for about 7 minutes, shaking the basket every 2 minutes.
6. Once the popping has stopped, transfer to a bowl and toss with your chosen topping. Serve immediately.

43

CHAPTER 7

PECAN PIE BAKED OATS

Prep time: 5 minutes | **Cook time:** 10 minutes | **Serves** 1

- 150ml milk
- 15g chia seeds or ground linseeds
- 20g maple syrup or clear honey
- 60g porridge oats
- 25g pecan halves
- 1 teaspoon vanilla extract
- Pinch of salt

1. Combine all ingredients in a heatproof dish that fits your air fryer.
2. Place the dish in the air fryer. Cook at 170°C for 10 minutes (no preheating required). Serve hot.

SWEET 'N' SPICY SWEET-POTATO CHIPS

Prep time: 10 minutes | **Cook time:** 15 minutes | **Serves** 5

- 2 large sweet potatoes, peeled
- 1 tablespoon olive oil
- 1 tablespoon smoked paprika
- 1 tablespoon garlic powder
- ½ tablespoon light brown sugar
- ½ tablespoon onion powder
- ½ teaspoon chili powder
- 1 teaspoon sea salt
- 1 teaspoon freshly ground black pepper

1. Using a mandoline or sharp knife, slice the sweet potatoes into very thin rounds.
2. In a large bowl, toss the sweet potato slices with olive oil until thoroughly coated. Add the remaining ingredients and toss well.
3. Arrange the slices in the air fryer basket without overlapping. Cook in batches at 200°C until crispy, about 12 minutes.

TASTY SIDES AND SNACKS

BAKED GOAT'S CHEESE POTS

Prep time: 5 minutes | **Cook time:** 15 minutes | **Serves** 4

- 15g butter, for greasing
- 200g goat's cheese log (with rind), cut into 12 slices
- 200g crème fraîche
- ½ teaspoon salt
- ¼ teaspoon freshly ground black pepper
- 30g walnuts, roughly chopped
- 2 teaspoons fresh flat-leaf parsley, chopped
- 2 eating apples, thinly sliced, to serve
- Crusty bread, to serve
- 4 ramekins

1. Butter the ramekins and place three slices of goat's cheese in the base of each.
2. Mix the crème fraîche with salt and pepper, then divide equally between the ramekins. Top with the chopped walnuts.
3. Preheat the air fryer to 160°C. Cook the ramekins for 12 minutes.
4. Scatter with parsley and serve with apple slices and crusty bread.

CHILLI AND PAPRIKA ROOT VEGETABLE CRISPS

Prep time: 10 minutes | **Cook time:** 28 minutes | **Serves** 4

- 1 small sweet potato, scrubbed
- 1 beetroot, scrubbed
- 1 parsnip, scrubbed
- 2 teaspoons chilli-flavoured oil
- 2 teaspoons smoked paprika, plus extra for sprinkling
- 1 teaspoon sea salt

1. Using a mandoline or sharp knife, slice the vegetables very thinly (about 2.5mm thick). Place in a large bowl, add the oil and toss to coat. Add the paprika and salt and toss again.
2. Working in batches, arrange half the vegetable slices in a single layer in the preheated air fryer at 150°C. Cook for 12 minutes, turning halfway through. Remove any crisps that are golden, then cook the remainder for 1-2 minutes more until golden. Transfer to a wire rack to crisp up as they cool. Repeat with the remaining vegetables.
3. Sprinkle with extra paprika before serving.

CHAPTER 8: CLASSICAL & SIMPLE

CLASSICAL & SIMPLE

GARLIC PRAWN STARTER

Prep time: 10 minutes | **Cook time:** 15 minutes | **Serves** 3

- 450g of raw prawns, ready to cook
- Cooking oil spray
- ¼ teaspoon garlic powder
- Salt and pepper to taste
- Fresh lemon wedges
- Optional: chopped parsley and/or chilli flakes to garnish

1. Preheat the air fryer to 200°C.
2. Add the oil, garlic powder, salt, and pepper into one bowl and mix. Add the prawns and toss in the seasoned oil until thoroughly coated.
3. Put the prawns into the air fryer and cook at 200°C for 10–14 minutes. Pause cooking and shakes a couple of times throughout.
4. Serve the garlic prawns on a bed of lettuce with a squeeze of fresh lemon, and a sprinkle of parsley and chilli flakes.

SQUASH WITH BLUE CHEESE DRESSING

Prep time: 5 minutes | **Cook time:** 25 minutes | **Serves** 2

- ½ squash, around 400g, peeled and cut into 2cm
- 1 tablespoon extra-virgin olive oil
- 1 radicchio, leaves separated
- salt and pepper

For The Dressing:
- 60g soured cream
- 70g blue cheese
- 3 tablespoons Greek yogurt
- 1 teaspoon lemon juice

1. Preheat the air fryer to 180°C for 4 minutes.
2. Put the squash into a medium-sized bowl, drizzle over the olive oil and season well with salt and pepper. Put it into the air fryer and cook for around 20 minutes until tender and starting to char.
3. Meanwhile, place all the dressing ingredients into a small blender and blitz until smooth.
4. Serve by mixing together the radicchio and squash, then tossing with the dressing.

CHAPTER 8

GARLIC BUTTER SALMON WITH GREEN BEANS

Prep time: 10 minutes | **Cook time:** 10 minutes | **Serves** 4

- 5 garlic cloves, finely chopped
- 15g of parmesan cheese, grated
- Juice of 1 lemon
- 1 teaspoon of Italian herb seasoning (shop bought or make your own)
- 60g/2oz of melted butter
- Pinch of coarse sea salt
- 300g of fresh green beans
- 4 salmon fillets, approximately 170g each
- Olive oil cooking spray
- Ground black pepper
- Optional: torn fresh parsley

1. Mix the garlic, parmesan, lemon juice, Italian seasoning, and melted butter together in a bowl, and season with salt.
2. Cut four sheets of baking paper big enough to place a piece of salmon with extra around to fold over.
3. Divide the green beans evenly between the 4 sheets of baking paper and spray lightly with the cooking oil.
4. Place the salmon fillets on top of the green beans and brush with the garlic butter sauce. Season with freshly ground pepper.
5. Preheat the air fryer to 180°C.
6. Fold the sheets in half across each piece of salmon and roll the remaining sides up to create four neat little parcels. Place each parcel carefully in the air fryer.
7. Cook at 180°C for about 8-10 minutes or until cooked through.
8. Once cooked, remove from the parcel, garnish with parsley and a little more parmesan.
9. Serve immediately.

GARLIC BREAD

Prep time: 5 minutes | **Cook time:** 10 minutes | **Serves** 2

- 4 slices of ciabatta
- 3 garlic cloves, crushed
- a few pinches of dried parsley
- 4 tablespoons freshly grated hard cheese
- 15 g butter, melted

1. Preheat the air fryer to 180°C.
2. Mix the garlic, parsley and cheese into the melted butter. Spread the garlic butter onto the ciabatta slices. Pop the slices into the preheated air fryer and cook for 3–5 minutes or until cooked to your liking. Eat hot.
3. NOTE: To melt butter in an air fryer, preheat the air fryer to 160°C. Pop the butter into a ramekin or heatproof dish, then place in the preheated air fryer for 2-3 minutes until melted.

CLASSICAL & SIMPLE

ROASTED BEETS AND PARSNIPS WITH TAHINI DRESSING

Prep time: 15 minutes | **Cook time:** 30 minutes | **Serves** 4

- 800g mixed beets and parsnips, peeled and cut into 1-inch chunks
- 2 tbsp olive oil
- 1 tsp ground cumin
- 1 tsp dried thyme
- Salt and black pepper to taste

- **For the Tahini Dressing:**
- 3 tbsp tahini
- 2 tbsp lemon juice
- 1 garlic clove, minced
- 2 tbsp water
- Salt and pepper to taste

1. Preheat the air fryer to 200°C.
2. In a large bowl, toss the beet and parsnip chunks with the olive oil, cumin, thyme, salt, and pepper until evenly coated.
3. Spread the vegetables out in a single layer in the air fryer basket. Cook for 25-30 minutes, shaking the basket halfway, until the vegetables are tender and starting to caramelize.
4. Meanwhile, make the tahini dressing. In a small bowl, whisk together the tahini, lemon juice, garlic, and water until smooth. Season with salt and pepper to taste.
5. Transfer the roasted beets and parsnips to a serving dish. Drizzle the tahini dressing over the top and toss gently to coat.
6. Serve warm, garnished with chopped fresh parsley or thyme if desired. This makes a great side dish or can be enjoyed as a main course.

FRIED OLIVES

Prep time: 10 minutes | **Cook time:** 10 minutes | **Serves** 4

- 1 x 280g/10oz jar stuffed green olives
- 255g/9oz of breadcrumbs
- 85g/3oz plain flour
- ½ teaspoon of garlic powder
- ½ teaspoon of paprika or chilli powder
- 3 eggs
- Olive oil cooking spray

1. Start with 3 bowls. Crack the egg into the first bowl and whisk. Mix the flour, paprika and garlic powder in the second bowl. Put the breadcrumbs into the third bowl.
2. Drain and dry the olives and toss them in the flour.
3. Next, dip the olives in the bowl of beaten egg, coating them well.
4. Finally, turn the olives in the breadcrumb mixture so they are completely covered, then place them in a single layer onto a plate.
5. Spray the olives with the cooking oil and give the air fryer a light spritz of oil too.
6. Arrange the olives in the air fryer with plenty of space between them.
7. Preheat the air fryer to 200°C/400F, then air fry them for 5 minutes.
8. Turn the olives, spray them with cooking spray, and air fry for a further 3 minutes.
9. Transfer them to a plate.
10. Delicious served with a fresh oregano garnish and/or sprinkled with parmesan cheese.
11. Eat with your favourite dipping sauce.

CHAPTER 8

VEGGIE BURGERS

Prep time: 10 minutes | **Cook time: 10 minutes** | **Serves 4**

- 500g of sweet potato
- 800g of cauliflower
- 200g of carrots
- 170g of chickpeas, drained
- 240g of breadcrumbs
- 100g of grated mozzarella
- 15g of dried mixed herbs
- 15g of basil
- Salt and pepper to taste

1. Peel and chop the vegetables into small pieces. Steam until tender.
2. Drain and dry any moisture from the vegetables so that they are dry.
3. Add the chickpeas to the vegetables and mash together so they are well combined.
4. Mix in the breadcrumbs and seasonings. Shape into burgers.
5. Pre heat the air fryer to 180°C.
6. Roll in the mozzarella so the burgers are completely covered in grated cheese.
7. Line the air fryer and spritz with a little cooking oil spray as the cheese will melt, then put the burgers in.
8. Cook at 180°C for 10 minutes. Turn the temperature to 200°C and cook for another until crusty on the outside.
9. Serve in burger buns with a side of salad.

CARIBBEAN BONE-FREE JACKFRUIT "PORK" CHOPS

Prep time: 30 minutes | **Cook time: 10 minutes** | **Serves 2**

- 2 bone-free pork chops about 170g each
- 30ml of olive oil
- 1 teaspoon of light brown sugar
- 40g of jerk seasoning (use less if you prefer a less spicy meal)
- Salt to taste

1. Combine the brown sugar, jerk seasoning, and salt until blended. Set to one side.
2. Lightly spray both sides of the pork shops then coat all over with the seasoning rub, cover, and leave to marinate for 30 minutes.
3. Preheat the air fryer to 190°C and lightly spray with oil.
4. Put the seasoned pork chops into the air fryer and cook at 190°C for 5-6 minutes. Turn the pork chops and cook for another 5-6 at the same temperature.
5. When cooked, transfer to a place and allow to rest for 5 minutes.
6. Serve with a tossed salad, rice, or pasta.

50

CLASSICAL & SIMPLE

COURGETTE PIZZA SLICES

Prep time: 5 minutes | **Cook time:** 11 minutes | **Serves** 2

- ½ medium courgette/courgette
- Extra-virgin olive oil spray
- 4 tsp dried oregano
- 3 tbsp light cream cheese
- 28g grated Cheddar cheese
- Salt and black pepper

1. Slice the courgettes into 6mm/¼in thick slices (I usually get around 12 slices from a medium courgette) and spray the tops with olive oil. Sprinkle with half the dried oregano and season with salt and pepper.
2. Place the slices in the air fryer, spreading them out so that none are on top of each other. Air fry at 180°C for 8 minutes, or until soft in the middle and starting to get crispy.
3. Remove the courgette slices and spread them with cream cheese. Sprinkle with grated cheese and press it down into the cream cheese so that it doesn't fly away, then finish by sprinkling over the remaining oregano.
4. Return the courgette slices to the air fryer and cook at 200°C for a final 3 minutes to melt the cheese.

CHARRED CORN SALSA SALAD

Prep time: 5 minutes | **Cook time:** 25 minutes | **Serves** 2

For The Corn:
- 4 corn cobs
- Olive oil spray

For The Salsa:
- 300g vine tomatoes, cut into chunks
- 1 avocado, cut into 2cm pieces
- 1 spring onion, finely sliced
- 225g roasted red peppers, cut into strips
- ½ red onion, finely sliced
- 1 red chilli, deseeded and finely chopped
- Juice of 1 lime
- 15g fresh coriander leaves
- 2 tbsp extra-virgin olive oil
- Salt and pepper

1. Preheat the air fryer to 200°C for 4 minutes.
2. Place the corn cobs in the air fryer, spray with a little oil, and cook for 15 minutes. Flip, spray with more oil, and cook for 10 more minutes until charred.
3. Meanwhile, combine all the salsa ingredients in a bowl. Season with salt and pepper.
4. Cut the charred corn kernels off the cobs and mix into the salsa.
5. Serve the corn salsa salad immediately.

CHAPTER 9: WEEKEND FEASTS

WEEKEND FEASTS

ORZO WITH PRAWNS & SALSA VERDE

Prep time: 5 minutes | **Cook time:** 20 minutes | **Serves** 2

- 160g orzo
- 1 tablespoon 'nduja
- 1 tablespoon butter
- 160g raw king prawns
- Salt and freshly ground black pepper

For the Salsa Verde:

- 15g flat-leaf parsley
- 10g basil leaves
- 5g mint leaves
- 1 tablespoon capers
- 1 anchovy fillet
- 4 tablespoons extra-virgin olive oil
- 1 tablespoon red wine vinegar
- 1 teaspoon caster sugar
- Salt and freshly ground black pepper

1. Bring a large pot of water to the boil and season generously with salt. Once boiling, add the orzo and cook according to packet instructions. Drain and transfer to a 19cm baking dish that fits into your air fryer.
2. Preheat the air fryer to 170°C for 4 minutes.
3. Dot the 'nduja and butter over the orzo, then cook for 2 minutes. Season with salt and pepper, then stir.
4. Add the prawns and cook for a further 2 minutes until the prawns are cooked through and the orzo is turning slightly crisp on top.
5. Meanwhile, finely chop the parsley, basil, mint, capers and anchovy, then add to a small bowl with the oil, red wine vinegar and sugar. Season with salt and mix well.
6. Serve the orzo with the salsa verde spooned over.

TANDOORI CHICKEN BREAST FILLET

Prep time: 30 minutes | **Cook time:** 60 minutes | **Serves** 4

- 800g skin-on, bone-in chicken breast fillet
- 1½ teaspoons salt
- 280g plain Greek yoghurt
- 2 garlic cloves, finely chopped
- 15g sweet paprika
- 2 teaspoons ground turmeric
- 2.5cm piece fresh root ginger, grated
- 1 teaspoon ground cumin
- Olive oil cooking spray

1. Pat the chicken dry with kitchen roll, then season with 1 teaspoon of the salt (save ½ teaspoon for the marinade.) Set aside.
2. Combine the yoghurt, garlic, paprika, turmeric, ginger, cumin, and remaining ½ teaspoon salt together in a bowl.
3. Cover the chicken all over with the chicken mixture. Allow to stand at room temperature for about 30 minutes.
4. Preheat the air fryer to 180°C. Spray with cooking oil.
5. Put the marinated chicken in the air fryer and cook at 180°C/350F for 35–40 minutes, turning every 10 minutes to ensure its golden brown all over and cooked through.
6. Remove the chicken from the fryer onto a plate and let rest about 10 minutes before slicing.
7. Serve as part of a main meal.

CHAPTER 9

THE COMPLETE AIR FRIED BARBECUE

Prep time: 10 minutes | **Cook time:** 60 minutes | **Serves** 4

- 4 beef burgers
- 6 good-quality sausages
- 3 pork steaks
- 3 thin beef steaks
- 500g baby potatoes
- 500g Mediterranean vegetables (courgettes, peppers, mushrooms)
- 30ml olive oil (divided into 2 × 15ml)
- 6g dried oregano
- 6g dried parsley
- Salt and freshly ground black pepper

1. Preheat the air fryer to 180°C and spray with cooking oil.
2. In a large bowl, toss the potatoes with 15ml of the olive oil and half of the seasonings. Ensure the potatoes are coated well.
3. Place the potatoes in the air fryer and cook for 17 minutes at 180°C.
4. Take the baby potatoes out of the air fryer and keep them warm.
5. Put the 4 burgers and 4 sausages into the air fryer and cook for 10 minutes at 180°C. Remove and keep warm once cooked.
6. Put the remaining 2 sausages, the pork steaks and however many of the beef steaks that will fit without overcrowding. Cook for 10 minutes at 180°C.
7. Meanwhile, add the Mediterranean vegetables to a bowl with the remaining oil and seasoning and coat well. Once the steaks are cooked, remove them from the air fryer and load with the vegetables. Cook for another 12 minutes at 180°C.
8. Finally, when the vegetables are cooked, transfer them to a warmed bowl and add the last of the steaks. Cook for 6 minutes at 180°C.
9. Plate up and serve!

WEEKEND FEASTS

BUTTERMILK-MARINATED ROAST CHICKEN

Prep time: 30 minutes | **Cook time:** 60 minutes | **Serves** 4

- 1.4kg whole chicken, trimmed
- 2 teaspoons sea salt (for pre-seasoning)
- 475ml buttermilk
- Salt and freshly ground black pepper

1. Twenty-four hours before cooking, season the chicken with 2 teaspoons of sea salt and leave for 30 minutes. Truss the legs with kitchen string.
2. Place the salted chicken in a large bowl and pour over the buttermilk. Cover tightly and refrigerate overnight, turning once to ensure even marinating.
3. The next day, preheat the air fryer to 180°C.
4. Remove the chicken from the buttermilk, discarding the marinade. Place the chicken breast-side down in the air fryer basket. Season well with salt and pepper.
5. Cook for 25 minutes.
6. Turn the chicken breast-side up, season again, and cook for a further 25 minutes until golden brown and the juices run clear when pierced at the thickest part.
7. Transfer to a warm plate and rest for 10 minutes before carving.

DOM'S WEEKNIGHT MEAT PIZZA

Prep time: 10 minutes | **Cook time:** 17 minutes | **Serves** 2

- 450g minced beef
- 3 tablespoons light cream cheese
- 1 teaspoon dried oregano
- 1 teaspoon dried basil
- Salt and freshly ground black pepper

For the Toppings:

- 1½ tablespoons tomato purée
- 1½ teaspoons garlic purée
- 115g grated mozzarella
- 6 cherry tomatoes
- Pinch of dried oregano

1. Mix the minced beef, cream cheese, oregano and basil in a bowl and season with salt and pepper. Combine well with your hands, then form into a large ball. Set aside.
2. Line the air fryer basket with foil, folding down the edges to create a pizza pan shape. Place in the basket.
3. Place the meat mixture onto the foil and flatten with your hands to create a base about 1cm thick.
4. Mix the tomato and garlic purées together and spread evenly over the meat base. Air fry at 180°C (360°F) for 10 minutes, or until the meat reaches 60°C on a thermometer.
5. Sprinkle with mozzarella, halved cherry tomatoes and oregano.
6. Air fry at 180°C for a further 7 minutes, until the cheese has melted. Slice and serve.

55

CHAPTER 9

FAMILY FAVOURITES ROAST LAMB

Prep time: 10 minutes | **Cook time:** 1 hour 20 minutes | **Serves** 4

- 1.2kg lamb joint
- 300g potatoes, peeled and cut for roasting
- 15ml olive oil
- 2 teaspoons fresh rosemary
- 1 teaspoon fresh thyme
- 1 teaspoon bouquet garni
- Salt and freshly ground black pepper

1. Preheat the air fryer to 160°C and spray with oil.
2. Use a sharp knife to score the lambs skin and season with the salt, pepper, bouquet garni and thyme, paying extra attention to the score marks.
3. Put the joint in the air fryer and cook at 160°C for about 30 minutes.
4. Toss the potatoes in a separate bowl with salt, pepper, rosemary, and olive oil. Use your hands to mix well and ensure the potatoes are well coated.
5. Turn the lamb after the 30 minutes and place the seasoned potatoes in the gaps around the lamb joint. Cook for another 25 minutes at 160°C.
6. Check the lamb at the end of cooking, and if it looks too pink in the middle, cook for a few minutes longer.
7. Finally, remove the potatoes and keep warm while the lamb 'rests' for 10 minutes.
8. Carve the lamb and serve with roast potatoes and seasonal vegetables.

MARINADED FILIPINO-STYLE BARBECUE CHICKEN

Prep time: 10 minutes | **Cook time:** 50 minutes | **Serves** 4

- 1.4kg chicken, butterflied to even thickness
- 120ml light soy sauce
- 60ml lemon juice
- 115g soft brown sugar
- 1 whole garlic bulb, peeled and finely chopped
- 1 teaspoon salt
- 1 teaspoon freshly ground black pepper
- Cooking oil spray

1. Combine the soy sauce, lemon juice, brown sugar, garlic, salt and pepper in a bowl and mix thoroughly to make the marinade. Remove about 1/3 of the marinade and set aside to use later.
2. Add the chicken to the bowl and rub all over with the marinade to ensure it's thoroughly coated. Cover the bowl and leave the chicken to marinate for at least 4 hours in the fridge.
3. Remove from the fridge at least 30 hours before cooking.
4. Preheat the air fryer to 180°C and line with lightly greased foil.
5. Drain the chicken and discard any marinade. Place the chicken in the air fryer and spray with cooking oil so it doesn't dry out while cooking.
6. Place the saved marinade in a small pan and bring to the boil. Simmer gently for a few minutes.
7. Cook for about 15 minutes on 180°C. Turn the chicken, spray with a little more oil and cook for another 15–20 minutes until cooked through.
8. Remove to a platter, pour over the remaining marinade/sauce and allow to rest for 10 minutes before serving.

WEEKEND FEASTS

CHILLI CON CARNE

Prep time: 10 minutes | **Cook time:** 45 minutes | **Serves** 6

- 1 onion, finely chopped
- 400g tin chopped tomatoes
- 1 fresh red chilli, deseeded and finely chopped (optional)
- 350ml hot beef stock
- 30g tomato purée
- Salt and freshly ground black pepper
- Chilli powder to taste (start with ½ teaspoon)
- 1 teaspoon ground coriander
- 1 teaspoon ground cumin
- 500g lean minced beef
- 15ml olive oil
- 1 red pepper, deseeded and diced
- 400g tin red kidney beans, drained and rinsed
- 150g sweetcorn

1. Preheat the air fryer to 180°C.
2. Place the onion, red pepper and chillies into the air fryer basket, drizzle with oil and cook for 5 minutes.
3. Add the minced beef, breaking up any large chunks with a wooden spoon. Cook for another 5 minutes until the meat is browned.
4. In a small bowl, combine the spices and seasoning with the tomato purée and 200ml of the beef stock. Reserve the remaining 150ml of stock.
5. Pour the spiced stock mixture into the air fryer along with the tinned tomatoes. Stir well and cook for 25 minutes, stirring occasionally.
6. Add the kidney beans and remaining hot beef stock, stirring to combine.
7. Cook for a further 5-10 minutes until thoroughly heated.
8. Serve with fluffy white rice and a dollop of soured cream.

STICKY PORK RIBS WITH HONEY AND GARLIC

Prep time: 10 minutes | **Cook time:** 40 minutes | **Serves** 6

- 1kg pork spare ribs
- 115g clear honey
- 60ml light soy sauce
- 60g tomato ketchup
- 60g soft brown sugar
- 30ml rice wine vinegar
- 30ml lemon juice
- 2 teaspoons toasted sesame oil
- 4 garlic cloves, finely chopped
- 10g sesame seeds, to garnish (optional)
- 30g spring onions, finely sliced (optional)

1. For the marinade, combine the honey, soy sauce, ketchup, brown sugar, vinegar and lemon juice in a large bowl.
2. Reserve one-third of the marinade in a jug and refrigerate.
3. Coat the pork ribs in the remaining marinade, cover and leave to marinate overnight in the fridge.
4. Preheat the air fryer to 190°C. Line with greased foil.
5. Remove the ribs from the fridge 30 minutes before cooking to reach room temperature.
6. Arrange the ribs in a single layer in the air fryer and cook for 10-12 minutes, turning once.
7. Meanwhile, heat a large frying pan or wok over medium heat. Sauté the garlic in sesame oil for 1 minute, then add the reserved marinade. Heat gently, stirring continuously until thickened.
8. Once cooked, toss the ribs in the thickened sauce with the sesame seeds and garnish with spring onions to serve.

CHAPTER 9

CLASSIC BANGERS AND MASH WITH ONION GRAVY

Prep time: 10 minutes | Cook time: 45 minutes | Serves 6

For the Bangers:
- 6 Cumberland sausages
- 15ml olive oil

For the Mash:
- 1kg Maris Piper potatoes, peeled and cut into chunks
- 50g unsalted butter
- 100ml whole milk
- Sea salt and freshly ground black pepper

For the Onion Gravy:
- 30g unsalted butter
- 2 large onions, thinly sliced
- 15g plain flour
- 300ml beef stock
- 15ml Worcestershire sauce
- 5g soft brown sugar

1. Preheat the air fryer to 200°C.
2. Place the sausages in the air fryer basket and cook for 15-20 minutes, turning halfway through, until golden brown and cooked through.
3. Meanwhile, for the mash, place the potatoes in a large pan of cold, salted water. Bring to the boil and simmer for 15-20 minutes until tender.
4. For the gravy, melt the butter in a large frying pan over medium heat. Add the onions and cook for 10-15 minutes until soft and caramelised, stirring occasionally.
5. Sprinkle flour over the onions and cook for 1 minute. Gradually add the stock, Worcestershire sauce and brown sugar, stirring constantly. Simmer for 5-7 minutes until thickened.
6. Drain the potatoes and return to the pan. Add the butter and warm milk, then mash until smooth. Season well with salt and pepper.
7. Serve the sausages on a bed of creamy mash, topped with the onion gravy. Accompany with garden peas if desired.

CHAPTER 10: SAUCES & HOMEMADE ESSENTIALS

CHAPTER 10

ROASTED AUBERGINE MEDITERRANEO

Prep time: 10 minutes | Cook time: 45 minutes | Serves 2

- 1 large aubergine, pricked with a fork
- 2 garlic cloves, minced
- 60g Bulgarian feta cheese, crumbled
- 1 tsp fresh oregano, chopped
- 1 tsp fresh mint, chopped
- 60ml fresh lemon juice
- 1 beefsteak tomato or 2 plum tomatoes, cored and finely chopped
- 60g black olives (e.g., Kalamata or Gaeta), pitted and chopped
- ½ tsp sea salt
- ¼ tsp black pepper

1. Preheat the oven to 225 °C.
2. Place the aubergine on a baking sheet in the oven and roast, turning often, until it is very soft when pricked with a fork, about 45 minutes. When it is cool enough to handle, scoop out the flesh, place in a large mixing bowl, and coarsely mash. Discard the skin.
3. Add the remaining ingredients and stir until just blended.

SPICY KETCHUP

Prep time: 10 minutes | Cook time: 30 minutes | Serves 4

- 15g unsalted butter
- 2 medium white onions, finely chopped
- 1 tin chopped tomatoes
- 100g light brown sugar
- 120ml white vinegar
- 1 tsp ground allspice

1. In a large skillet, melt the butter over medium heat. Add the onions and cook, stirring occasionally, until caramelized, about 23 minutes.
2. Add the tomatoes, brown sugar, vinegar, and allspice. Reduce heat to medium-low and cook, stirring occasionally, until reduced by half, about 30 minutes.
3. Remove from heat and let cool. Pour into a blender and process until smooth. Chill for 30–60 minutes before serving.

SAUCES & HOMEMADE ESSENTIALS

SWEET AND SOUR SAUCE

Prep time: 5 minutes | **Cook time:** 5 minutes | **Serves** 2

- 60g sugar
- 2 tbsp white or rice vinegar
- 2 tbsp ketchup
- 1 tbsp soy sauce
- 1 tsp cornflour
- 2 tbsp water

1. In a small saucepan, combine the sugar, vinegar, ketchup, soy sauce, cornstarch, and water.
2. Stir until well combined and smooth.
3. Bring the mixture to a boil over medium heat.
4. Reduce heat and simmer for 5-7 minutes, or until the sauce has thickened.

HONEY MUSTARD SAUCE

Prep time: 5 minutes | **Cook time:** 5 minutes | **Serves** 2

- 60ml honey
- 2 tbsp Dijon mustard
- 2 tbsp mayonnaise
- 1 tbsp lemon juice

1. In a small bowl, whisk together the honey, Dijon mustard, mayonnaise, and lemon juice until smooth.

SPICY GARLIC PARMESAN SAUCE

Prep time: 5 minutes | **Cook time:** 5 minutes | **Serves** 2

- 2 tbsp olive oil
- 3 garlic cloves, minced
- 60g grated Parmesan
- ½ tsp red pepper flakes
- ¼ tsp sea salt
- ⅛ tsp black pepper

1. Heat the olive oil in a small saucepan over medium heat.
2. Add the minced garlic and cook until fragrant, about 30 seconds.
3. Stir in the Parmesan cheese, red pepper flakes, salt, and pepper.
4. Let simmer for 2-3 minutes, or until the sauce is heated through and the Parmesan cheese is melted.

BBQ SAUCE

Prep time: 5 minutes | **Cook time:** 15 minutes | **Serves** 2

- 120ml ketchup
- 60g brown sugar
- 60ml apple cider vinegar
- 1 tbsp Worcestershire sauce
- 1 tsp mustard powder
- ½ tsp liquid smoke

1. In a small saucepan, combine the ketchup, brown sugar, apple cider vinegar, Worcestershire sauce, mustard powder, and liquid smoke.
2. Bring the mixture to a simmer over medium heat.
3. Reduce heat and let simmer for 10-15 minutes, or until the sauce has thickened.

CHAPTER 10

SOUR CREAM & BACON DIP

Prep time: 3 minutes | **Cook time:** 16 minutes | **Serves** m4

- 2 rashers streaky bacon
- 120ml sour cream
- 1 tsp dried chives
- Salt and black pepper

1. Place the bacon in the air fryer basket and cook at 180°C for 8 mins. Turn the bacon and cook for another 8 mins, or until crispy.
2. Allow to cool, then crush the bacon in a food bag with a rolling pin.
3. Combine bacon crumbs with sour cream and chives in a bowl. Season with salt and pepper, and mix with a fork.

BASIC HOMEMADE BREADCRUMBS

Prep time: 10 minutes | **Cook time:** 15 minutes | **Serves** 4

- Fresh or stale (but not rock-hard) bread

1. If using fresh bread, preheat the air fryer to 150°C. Slice the bread and arrange it in a single layer in the air fryer basket. Toast for 8–10 mins, or until crisp, checking halfway to avoid over-browning. Allow to cool.
2. Cut the bread into 5cm chunks and place in a food processor (in batches, if necessary). Process until breadcrumbs are about the size of rice grains. Alternatively, place the bread chunks in a plastic bag and crush them with a rolling pin until they reach the desired size.
3. Store in an airtight container in the fridge for up to 1 month.

HOMEMADE GARLIC BUTTER

Prep time: 5 minutes | **Cook time:** 15 minutes | **Serves** 2

- 100g unsalted butter, softened
- 3 cloves garlic, minced
- 1 tbsp fresh parsley, finely chopped (optional)
- A pinch of sea salt
- A pinch of black pepper
- 1 tsp lemon juice (optional)

1. In a small bowl, mix the softened butter and garlic together until well combined.
2. Stir in the parsley, salt, pepper, and lemon juice (if using).
3. Spoon the garlic butter onto a sheet of cling film or parchment paper, and shape it into a log. Wrap it tightly and refrigerate for 30 minutes to firm up.
4. Once set, slice the garlic butter as needed.

CREAMY RANCH SAUCE

Prep time: 5 minutes | **Cook time:** 5 minutes | **Serves** 2

- 100g mayonnaise
- 100g buttermilk
- 60ml sour cream
- 1 packet (28g) dry ranch dressing mix
- ¼ tsp garlic powder
- ¼ tsp onion powder

1. In a medium bowl, combine the mayonnaise, buttermilk, sour cream, ranch dressing mix, garlic powder, and onion powder.
2. Whisk until smooth and creamy.

APPENDIX 1: MEASUREMENT CONVERSION CHART

MEASUREMENT CONVERSION CHART

VOLUME EQUIVALENTS(DRY)

US STANDARD	METRIC (APPROXIMATE)
1/8 teaspoon	0.5 mL
1/4 teaspoon	1 mL
1/2 teaspoon	2 mL
3/4 teaspoon	4 mL
1 teaspoon	5 mL
1 tablespoon	15 mL
1/4 cup	59 mL
1/2 cup	118 mL
3/4 cup	177 mL
1 cup	235 mL
2 cups	475 mL
3 cups	700 mL
4 cups	1 L

WEIGHT EQUIVALENTS

US STANDARD	METRIC (APPROXIMATE)
1 ounce	28 g
2 ounces	57 g
5 ounces	142 g
10 ounces	284 g
15 ounces	425 g
16 ounces (1 pound)	455 g
1.5 pounds	680 g
2 pounds	907 g

VOLUME EQUIVALENTS(LIQUID)

US STANDARD	US STANDARD (OUNCES)	METRIC (APPROXIMATE)
2 tablespoons	1 fl.oz.	30 mL
1/4 cup	2 fl.oz.	60 mL
1/2 cup	4 fl.oz.	120 mL
1 cup	8 fl.oz.	240 mL
1 1/2 cup	12 fl.oz.	355 mL
2 cups or 1 pint	16 fl.oz.	475 mL
4 cups or 1 quart	32 fl.oz.	1 L
1 gallon	128 fl.oz.	4 L

TEMPERATURES EQUIVALENTS

FAHRENHEIT(F)	CELSIUS(C) (APPROXIMATE)
225 °F	107 °C
250 °F	120 °C
275 °F	135 °C
300 °F	150 °C
325 °F	160 °C
350 °F	180 °C
375 °F	190 °C
400 °F	205 °C
425 °F	220 °C
450 °F	235 °C
475 °F	245 °C
500 °F	260 °C

APPENDIX 2: THE DIRTY DOZEN AND CLEAN FIFTEEN

The Dirty Dozen and Clean Fifteen

The Environmental Working Group (EWG) is a nonprofit, nonpartisan organization dedicated to protecting human health and the environment Its mission is to empower people to live healthier lives in a healthier environment. This organization publishes an annual list of the twelve kinds of produce, in sequence, that have the highest amount of pesticide residue-the Dirty Dozen-as well as a list of the fifteen kinds ofproduce that have the least amount of pesticide residue-the Clean Fifteen.

THE DIRTY DOZEN

- The 2016 Dirty Dozen includes the following produce. These are considered among the year's most important produce to buy organic:

  - Strawberries
  - Apples
  - Nectarines
  - Peaches
  - Celery
  - Grapes
  - Cherries
  - Spinach
  - Tomatoes
  - Bell peppers
  - Cherry tomatoes
  - Cucumbers
  - Kale/collard greens
  - Hot peppers

- The Dirty Dozen list contains two additional itemskale/collard greens and hot peppers-because they tend to contain trace levels of highly hazardous pesticides.

THE CLEAN FIFTEEN

- The least critical to buy organically are the Clean Fifteen list. The following are on the 2016 list:

  - Avocados
  - Corn
  - Pineapples
  - Cabbage
  - Sweet peas
  - Onions
  - Asparagus
  - Mangos
  - Papayas
  - Kiw
  - Eggplant
  - Honeydew
  - Grapefruit
  - Cantaloupe
  - Cauliflower

- Some of the sweet corn sold in the United States are made from genetically engineered (GE) seedstock. Buy organic varieties of these crops to avoid GE produce.

APPENDIX 3: INDEX

A

anchovy fillet 23, 53

apricot jam 18

aubergine 36, 39, 60

B

beans 15, 31

beef 54, 55, 57

beef stock 25, 58

beetroot 28, 45

breadcrumbs 9, 11, 13, 29, 39, 41, 49

broccoli 28, 39

brown sugar 24, 31, 44, 50, 56, 57, 58, 60

C

carrots 25, 50

cauliflower 37, 50

chicken breast 29, 53

chicken wings 10, 11, 41

cornflour 21, 61

courgette 15, 38, 39

Cumberland sausages 38, 58

F

fish pie mix 30

fish sauce 31

H

hot sauce 10

hummus 21

J

jalapeño 26

jalapeño chillies 11

L

lamb 21, 25, 56

leek 21

lemon juice 11

lettuce leaves 32

linseeds 44

liquid smoke 61

M

mayonnaise 32, 36, 61, 62

mozzarella 9, 11, 50, 55

mushrooms 15, 36, 37, 39, 41

O

oats 16, 38, 44

Olive oil 41

oregano 35, 41, 42, 54, 55, 60

oyster sauce 21

P

paprika 11, 13, 17, 33, 35, 37, 38, 44, 53

parsley 48

pomegranate seeds 21

pork chops 50

pork loin chops 26

pork sausages 15

pork shoulder 21

pork spare ribs 57

pork steaks 24

pork tenderloin steak 24

prawns 47, 53

pumpkin 19

R

radicchio 47

ramekins 45

S

salmon 28, 48

sirloin steak 23

sole fillets 28

soy sauce 21, 56, 57

sunflower oil 16, 33

sweetcorn 15, 57

T

tuna 23, 30

turkey 26, 32

turkey breast 33

V

vanilla extract 42, 44

vegan gnocchi 35

vegetable oil 42

vegetable stock 31, 37

W

walnuts 45

wine 36, 42, 57

Worcestershire sauce 25, 58, 61

Y

yellow squash 39

yoghurt 53

yogurt 47

65

Hey there!

Wow, can you believe we've reached the end of this culinary journey together? I'm truly thrilled and filled with joy as I think back on all the recipes we've shared and the flavors we've discovered. This experience, blending a bit of tradition with our own unique twists, has been a journey of love for good food. And knowing you've been out there, giving these dishes a try, has made this adventure incredibly special to me.

Even though we're turning the last page of this book, I hope our conversation about all things delicious doesn't have to end. I cherish your thoughts, your experiments, and yes, even those moments when things didn't go as planned. Every piece of feedback you share is invaluable, helping to enrich this experience for us all.

I'd be so grateful if you could take a moment to share your thoughts with me, be it through a review on Amazon or any other place you feel comfortable expressing yourself online. Whether it's praise, constructive criticism, or even an idea for how we might do things differently in the future, your input is what truly makes this journey meaningful.

This book is a piece of my heart, offered to you with all the love and enthusiasm I have for cooking. But it's your engagement and your words that elevate it to something truly extraordinary.

Thank you from the bottom of my heart for being such an integral part of this culinary adventure. Your openness to trying new things and sharing your experiences has been the greatest gift.

Catch you later,

Cristi G. Piedra

Printed in Great Britain
by Amazon